ALL OUR TOMORROWS

by THE ETERNAL AUTHOR

NARRATOR: Norma C.

Words. What are they, but symbols of
what is in our hearts.

COPYRIGHT

Published in paperback, 2023, in association with:
JV Author Services
www.jvauthorservices.co.uk
jvpublishing@yahoo.com

ISBN: 9798399493503

ACKNOWLEDGEMENTS

To all the realms of spirit who entrusted me with their stories and messages. To Terry Doyle for awakening my soul. To Audrey Collier, sister, and soul mate. To Lorraine Lambert, my teacher and confidante who gave me courage when I doubted myself.

To all my earth angels (too many to mention by name) and to all who walk with me on my pathway, for without you, dear souls, these stories would not have been told.

PREFACE

Putting pen to paper has been an adventure into the unknown that I thought would never happen.

To reach the realms of becoming an author seemed a tall order. I would be out of my depth. But I didn't realise that my words were never going to be used and that others would dictate their messages and stories to me.

When spirits gently nudged me into being their 'storyteller,' it became a partnership, a time of wonderment.

I realised what a compliment I was being paid and what trust was being put into my hands – scary but joyous.

I am not a great orator, but spirit in their wisdom reminded me that 'the pen is mightier than the sword' and that my pen could slay more dragons of the psyche than an ordinary book.

So, my dear reader, see what awaits you on the next page.

Norma C.

1

I begin today by talking about dreams. Dreams, as you know, are our subconscious, telling us of our desires, fears, and longings. Believe in your dreams, for they are messages from the forces of good.

Dear reader, I begin my story. Well, maybe not a story, for it may be a truth lurking somewhere deep within your unconscious thoughts, just ready to break through at a conscious level.

My story begins.

One day not long ago, a young child, a lonely boy devoid of all human contact, fell asleep. He dreamed of many wonderful countries and exotic places. He saw colour and smelt the dusty places of his dreams.

At first, all the cities were empty of people. Then slowly, his dream began to fill up with people of different colours wearing different clothes and different animals pursued them. All was silent at first, but then the noises began – loud noises, soft noises, birds began to sing, and animals began to express themselves. Men began to talk, shout, and laugh at each other, and it seemed to him that his world was getting bigger and bigger.

He liked his new world. Oh, how he wanted to be part of this world. He longed to be connected, but how?

The dream continued. He stepped into what he thought was the future, for he saw himself as a grown man. He had stepped into his dream.

He saw himself talking to all these people. He knew all the different languages and visited all these wonderful places, yet how was this going to be? He hoped the dream would never end, for how was he to get there?

My dear readers, you who may or may not be at one with your dreams or believe in them. The dreams of the conscious and the subconscious are but a flash of light away. The flash of realisation, the thought of, 'Of course, why did I not see that before?' is the only response needed.

But how to get there? You will, my friend, but I digress.

The child, in his innocence, believed that only as an adult would his dreams come true.

To reach out and touch even a leaf on a tree may be the only connection that your soul needs. Your senses all cry to be nourished. What is holding you back? Dreams are longings of the soul.

Perhaps the parable I relate will leave you guessing and puzzling, as can your dreams. Call on your dreams, ask for them to be unravelled, and touch every topic in your dreams. Do not dismiss them as being silly, for deep within your subconscious is a wealth of insight into your future, the answer to your problems. It will be hard at first and time-consuming, but the rewards are many.

'How and why?' you ask. Is not your Father the Father of all of us? Not in a religious sense but as a loving voice that, if listened to, will comfort and speak only your truth?

To have a dream come true! Oh, the joy of that. But not as a small child, do not wait until later to see the knowledge inside you.

So, my parable (or is it your parable?)

Truth is there inside you. You only have to remember, for it is in remembering that we learn.

2

Today let my story begin with an old proverb. 'He that believes in me, yet he be good, yet his actions be worthy, if his heart be cold.'

How does that sit with you? Is it a contradiction of values? Is it a parody? Let us evaluate this.

On the one hand, on the outside, all seems well. All seems good and wholesome. But we who see all, even the darkest crevasses of men's souls, know and shrink from that man.

As a little child, you will not enter the kingdom of heaven until humility is yours, even as a pauper, even as a disciple of God. Life is not worth the living, for to be truly a child of God is to have the innocence of a living thereof, for to be truly a child of God is to have the innocence of a newborn babe. Not naïve, not of slow wit, not slothful, but as a bright and shining star that all who touch and bathe in its light are reborn.

How to become a star? 'Is it easy?' you may ask. 'Do all who wish to be a star become a star? Who controls the power to become that star?'

I DO.

That may seem harsh, and that may seem unfair. Is it fair? Does what you perceive in your life seem fair?

Go as a small child in all your innocence, in all your beliefs, and talk to God. Ask him what his needs are.

When you can do this, all the world, with the kingdom of God, is at your right hand.

Does that sound fair? Is that to your liking? Does your soul rejoice at this finding? I think not. You are a creature of infinite good. If only you could see each other as I do – see my world as I do, see the joy that could be attained as I do. Little children, you who have such possibilities, beauty, and demeanour, if only you could see through the dark mist of the soul what can be achieved, what love the world could share. I weep at your loss and at the lost opportunities. Does not the Father, does not your mother call to you in her hour of need? But the need goes unheeded.

My beloved children, I go now to prepare the place I promised you. Do not leave me alone. Do not turn your back on me, for I long to see you with me in paradise. He who is prepared, he who is ready, and he who loves the Father more than himself is truly a child of God. He who knows that to answer his calling, which sees the glory in all he surveys, only has to ask of Him, and then his needs are answered.

Do I make it sound so simple? It is simply my world and how yours can be.

I hear you cry, 'Nonsense. The world is a tough, cold place where all is a struggle.'

Dear one, the struggle is of your own making. Seek ye the Lord. Take all your struggles to him. Ask, and it shall be received. Labour not. Struggle not. To fight is not a good fight.

Dear ones, I encase you all with my love. Does that not bring you comfort, as a mother brings her love to a newborn? I am waiting to see your response. Do not keep me waiting. Rest on me, for I have a mighty arm and shoulder. I wait for you. Do not keep me waiting too long, for I grow weary at your loss.

3

This day was never meant to dawn. The day was to be the blackest day known to mankind. A day of such retribution, the like of which had never been seen before.

My tale is bleak. Doom and destruction were all about. The animals sensed this. They, in their wisdom, knew, but Man, in his infinite wisdom, was unprepared.

My story is a song of joy and hope, yet to believe in my song, one must leave all thoughts of bliss behind. One cannot foretell all the prophecies and foreboding that have gone before.

The journey begins on an ordinary day. The sun shone, the birds sang, and the cows mooed. But in the sky, a light shone. A light that had never been there before. Few saw it and those who did paid little attention to it. But one man saw it and it puzzled him. It worried him. He told others, but they laughed and ignored his warnings.

As the day grew on, the light became brighter. Others blamed 'sunspots', and others blamed pollution.

The man sought advice from a priest. He declared that perhaps all was not well but trust in him. He would say a prayer on his behalf.

Still troubled, the man sought advice from a politician. 'Be not troubled, my good man', said the politician. 'We have all the resources to deal with an emergency.'

Still not satisfied, he sought out a learned teacher. He declared that history would show that the constellations are out of sync, and this is just a way of correcting themselves.

Having his needs met, the man continued on his

way. But still, his thoughts troubled him. What if they were wrong? Perhaps they are right? What do I know of such things? They are the experts.

Then a sharp pain caught him in his heart. He gasped for breath. Was this going to be his last breath? What did he know? The thought that all his life, he depended on others knowing better than him struck him and panic filled him. Was it too late? Was it too late to tell others to seek to find out for yourself? The truth can be tainted. The truth can be twisted by other consciences.

Do you know the truth? The whole truth? Find out for yourself. Do not leave it to others, for the truth as they see it is not your truth.

Believe in that gut feeling. Your senses have a knowing when something is right for you.

Believe, if you will, the will of others. But does that lead you to 'their' belief system?

What of the truth that is good for you and only you? Be not persuaded by others. Seek your truth, live your truth, act your truth, and fall by your truth. For come the day when you are to gasp your last breath, will that be too late?

4

To judge or not to judge? That is the question.

How do we judge another? Why do we judge another? Is not the concept of judging a philosophy born out of ignorance? The haves and the have-nots play their games.

But we should not be led into the trap of conceit. Be aware of the failing of others. To clothe in the mantle of superiority is a judgement far greater than that of a fool. For what is he that sees others as lesser men but the bigot of his society?

To judge or not to judge. To see your brother or sister as an equal. He that can do so is a pearl beyond measure.

Does the Father love you any the less because of your failings? Does he see that, layer upon layer, what is in your soul? He judges you not. He sees only the child, the lonely child waiting to be loved.

'Loved by whom?' You may ask. We all have a need to reach out and touch another, but we choose not to, in case of rejection and in case we are judged.

Dear hearts, look further than the surface. Look deep into your soul and see the light. See what shines there. Let your light shine.

Courage, I say, is yours for the taking. Be as little children and shine your light, for children know no other way. Be the first in your place of work, in the avenue where you dwell, in the family or on the bus you travel on. See how many other 'lights' you can ignite. Go and reap the rewards of a 'warrior', a 'light warrior'. Set the world ablaze, for as you do, so your little light will grow also.

I set you a challenge. Be my 'light warrior'. Set the world ablaze. Make friends with your enemies, for in doing so, you and only you will see good in others.

This is not for the faint-hearted. Others will rebel and shy away from you. Pursue and move on to the next.

Those who do my bidding and accept my challenges will know such joy, happiness, and contentment. To them, the meaning of life is their realisation.

Have fun, dear children. Joy be yours.

5

The story I tell may be true. Then again, it may be a fable. You, my dear reader, must judge. It is not for me to tell or advise but for your conscience. I begin.

A long time ago, maybe before time as we know it, all on the Earth plane knew and dwelt in love, beauty and gentleness. Long before we grew suspicious of each other when our hearts were full of warmth and when the blessings of God's Earth were bestowed on us in such glorious profusion. The time is right. The time of telling is at hand.

Believe in your righteousness. For much that the Sages of old wrote, little did they believe that their dream of a utopia would continue for all who are awakened to the realities of this new world. Children believe that goodness is just a step away. They believe that all dreams that are dreamt are just as much a reality in the subconscious. They only have to be accepted into the conscious.

The truth I now relate is a belief system that maybe, just maybe, could one day come to pass. I prepare a parable for you.

One day, a young bride, having just betrothed her love, looks longingly at her beloved. She sees no flaws in his looks or his demeanour. She smiles. She has it all. Yet she knows that deep down, one day, they will part, and he will die and leave her. But then she realises that it is such a long time in the future that she dismisses it as her foolishness.

Time passes and they grow old, and she remembers that day many years ago when as a young bride, she had these sad thoughts.

Where did the time go? Where did the years go? They seemed to have slipped through her fingers like sand.

The time is now. Be in the moment, for that is all we have. Love in the moment, for this is all you have.

We have no future. Time is not on our side. Habits are the panacea of dreamers. I need to shout this aloud to wake up the sleepers.

I do not talk of doom but of a bright new day to live a full, beautiful life, one that you were given.

Waste not a moment on dull idle thoughts, for time will slip through your fingers like grains of sand. Beware that the sands of time do not run out for you.

How much time and how much sand is left for you?

6

My dear reader, gone are the days when you and I could touch each other with just a thought. Evolution has sought to outwit us. The journeying that we do, the living we do, is just a small part of who and why we are.

Many philosophers have argued amongst themselves, judge and be judged. Come the day when we all can and will see that maybe, just maybe, we will see the truth that is there in front of us.

Take heed, little people. Listen and be warned. For comes the day of such calamities when the world you know now will cease to exist.

I do not seek to alarm you. It is with a loving guiding hand that I declare this to you. Some people choose to ignore me, some will heed my warnings, and those that do will bear a heavy burden, for they are to support the rest.

I call on all 'light workers' to respond to this call. You, my dear souls, will and can save our beautiful world. I say ours because YOU and you alone are now the caretakers of the world I once made.

Reach out and touch as many souls as can listen. Do so with pride, search out those that would destroy her and show them the errors of their ways.

I bless all who hear my call. I echo this call down the annals of time. Listen to the animals, learn and watch them, for they have knowledge far greater than man.

I leave you now with a smile. Look out of your window. What do you see? Would you like to see that picture again? You choose. Can you make it better? Or perhaps tomorrow, it will have vanished. Do not despair. All is not lost, not yet.

Go now and enjoy the view. Relish in it, for it has been heaven-sent. Why would I not give my children the best that I can?

May the sun shine forever on you, and may love be at your door, but remember who put it there.

7

The day was hers, or so she thought. It had been quite an event, the marriage of her son to a dear delightful, now daughter-in-law. The sun shone, the sky was blue, and everything went as planned. Perfect, but something troubled her. A feeling of gloom and unease crept over her.

She disregarded this as the 'empty nest syndrome', for she had now lost her dear boy, her little treasure. But who or what was she now? Not a mother anymore, not the dutiful servant of a demanding child - the role she had longed to play all those years before she married.

She sighed. Who or what was she now? Her role had been taken away. The emptiness of her life hit her. No one now depended on her. What was she to become?

She shook herself. 'Other mothers have gone through this', she thought. 'I am not the first nor the last.' She smiled at this. Did not her mother go through this same feeling and not say anything to her? Nor would she, for it was the unwritten law that mothers bear their thoughts and longings upon themselves.

The years passed, and this day became a distant memory. Until one day, just by chance, she came across an old book she had had for many years. She opened it and out fell a poem. Sitting down to read this piece of paper, all memories and feelings of her son's wedding day flooded back to her. It began:

'Take heed of whom we love,
For tomorrow is just a promise of the love that is taken for granted.

For what if tomorrow does not come? Will love remain?
Those who never love, those who have lost, will love find them in the morn?
What of love? Is it a blessing?
Where do we find love?
We do not find love. We give it.'

After all these years of emptiness, she smiled, 'Love is in the giving', of course. Not to be taken, not in the expectation of being loved, for in giving love, we receive love.

So, my dear reader, take heart, when the world seems empty and cold, remember that LOVE and to be LOVED are not the same. For it's in the giving of ourselves to others that LOVE is returned to us.

8

Today we begin a new chapter, a new phase in the annals of time. Forgotten are those dreams that once we relied on, but then again, perhaps they were seen to be outmoded. The rituals that mankind tolerated seemed to us at this time a contradiction of the truth we now believe.

Some might say that progress is little more than a blockage or a diversion between man and God.

What do you believe, my friend? Is man at the threshold of a new beginning? Is God just a thought form? If so, where is God in all of this? Is he sitting in a far-distance galaxy playing the harp, leaving us mortals to struggle on the best way we know how? Look around you. What do you see? Death, decay, conflict, and strife? Are your eyes not yet open? Do you not see what is there before your eyes? Each day seems endless and pointless. Where has the joy of life gone, the sunshine times of your youth? Age means nothing to those that see through the mist of their reality.

Where are we going on this long road, on this pathway through eternity? Do we go alone? Can we travel alone, and do we have a choice in such matters?

We have a choice in this matter, for loneliness is not the wisest of bedfellows. You need never feel the emptiness of a heavy soul. Simply put your faith into that dream, that knowledge that your Father is always near.

Do not rely on distant dreams that call to you, that tease and beckon you, then lead you astray. Have faith and have the courage to go it alone. Self-reliance does not tolerate the indecisions of the fool. The courage that once bore man on the ocean of life can be and is still there, lying deep within your psyche. Go, Dear One, deep down, down to where that little spark resides and watch it grow.

Be at peace within that little space. Watch that space grow. See it grow until it expands and fills your whole being.

Rest easy now. I will slow the pace down, but be warned, be aware that life is not the struggle you think it is. You, you are fighting your own shadow. Just take my hand, for I am always there with you. Lean on me when the days are rough and arduous.

Dear Heart, I am waiting to be your friend. Do not keep me waiting. Why struggle when my arms are so strong?

9

What would you do if your brother, mother, neighbour, and child all perished in a holocaust or fire? How could, how would you come to terms with your loss? Would you wish that you, too, had perished? Or thank God for your survival?

Let's consider both aspects. To survive would seem like an act of God. To perish would seem like an act of God.

How come God gets the blame each time? Are we so little of stature that to lay blame at God's door is so easy?

The survivor could or would say, 'I was saved because I am here to do great works, those that perished, it was their time, and their number was up.'

Let us go deeper into this concept. How or why do disasters ever exist?

The world, as we know it, is an ever-changing compound of matter. The laws that govern it are of such a nature that it is balanced and true. When man intervenes and thinks he is in charge, the balance of nature is upset. These catastrophes are not revenge for man's interference. Not so that the animal kingdom seeks its own revenge, but nature herself seeks to redress the balance.

Think upon your own thought form in all of this. Struggle with your conscience and seek to understand the laws that govern this world. Is it not possible that we, that you, who dwell on the Earth plane are but children playing with toys and not understanding the instructions?

It is time to move into adulthood, to read again the instructions that we sent out many centuries ago. But 'Oh dear', I hear you cry. 'Not everybody can read.' Well, my friend, is it not time that you did? And for those who can read, how about teaching all the others?

10

It was spring. It was the season of rebirth. The days were long and sunny, yet the world seemed at odds with itself, for down the road near farmer Giles's henhouse, conflict was brewing.

In the pecking order of this world stood old farmer Giles. He was a gentleman of good age. A lonely old soul that had seen the seasons come and go. His life had been full and busy, yet today all was confusion.

His favourite hen had not laid for many days now, and it was his policy to slay any of his livestock that failed to perform to expectations.

What to do? It was just a hen, just another mangy piece of livestock. But this hen had been producing eggs for his table for many months, and he had relished each breakfast coming his way.

He looked at her with a sad misty eye, a feeling of being let down, of deep regret, for farmers are not supposed to get attached to the hens. The business of supply and demand, of pound, shillings, and pence, was what it was all about. He had never felt like this before, which surprised him. He had never considered or contemplated the power he had over his stock.

'I am judge and jury', he said. 'Just because I am in charge, does that give me the right to be the executioner?'

He walked away from the henhouse deep in thought. All these years, all these animals that I have slaughtered. How could I? What right had I? But business is business and money talks. The books must balance. But whose books, God's, or mine? The day wore on and long into the night, this thought would not leave him.

He fell asleep. He began to dream. In his dream, he was a small boy, timid, and rather a loner. How he longed to belong to a large family where he was loved and needed. Due to circumstances that he did not understand or care about, his life changed. He was placed in a large, robust family where noise and laughter surrounded him. But even in his dream, each member of this family slowly began to disappear until he was the only one left yet again.

He woke in a sweat, startled at the similarity of his life. What had he done? The logic in his being was no more.

'It would seem that I have murdered my fellow creatures just because they have two legs, just because I have the power to do so. Is it the only reason? Is that the justice of man's conscience?'

His regret was immense. He sat for a long time debating the realisation that just because 'I could, I did.' The night faded into dawn. The sun came up on another beautiful spring day. But today was not going to be like any other.

The hen still lives today.

11

Hello again, my dear friends. Who are you? Do you know, do you really know who you are? You have a name, a sound you are known by, the sound that, when chanted, awakes your interest.

There are many sounds in the universe, each with a meaning and a definition to the owner of that sound. Are you happy with the sound you have been given? Does it please you?

Stop and listen. Really listen when someone calls your name. It may seem dull and ordinary to you, but to others, it is a melody of infinite beauty. For does not the sound represent you?

Through the annals of time, music and rhythm have played a big part in the development of man, the universe, and the cosmos. We all breathe to a rhythm and love to a rhythm. Man has his seasons – birth and death only two of them.

'But where does this all lead to?' you ask. It is leading you to a place of beauty and tranquillity, the like of which you cannot imagine. But bide a while, while I reiterate my philosophy to you.

He that is born of man can and will rise again – rise to the heights he was destined to achieve. Simply put all thoughts of revenge, of self-seeking gratification, and look to the rhythm of a new order, the one that you seem to have forgotten.

For when love flows, when time is yours (and it is), the heart will beat to a different rhythm. All sounds become melodious. So sing, Dear Ones, sing your song in rhythm to nature's beat.

For is she not your constant companion? She knows a good tune, one that has stood the test of time. Tune into her rhythm, for in knowing her, we know ourselves.

12

As you may know, today may not be the best of times, it may even be the worst of times, but today IS.

'A profound statement,' I hear you say.

Today is the Lord's Day when all who can will try and do the best they can for those they meet on their way.

How is the day going for you? A good one or a bad one? You choose. You can, you know. The choices are in your hands.

Circumstances may provide for the obvious, but, the choices are ours for the making.

'But what of bad fortune? Things beyond our control?' I hear you wail.

Are they beyond your control? Is the universe telling you something about the choices you have made in the past and not listened to?

This may sound glib, not a thought that can be easily entertained. But stop and think for just a moment. Realise that just maybe, our actions, just one slip of the tongue, one wrong move, started a cacophony of events so remote that the connection seems too trivial to contemplate.

But my Dear Hearts, take heed. Next time you feel that 'today is not one of my better days', go back. Retrace the events that led up to your mode of thinking. Could events have been different? Did I presume wrongly? Should I have delayed my journey?

But LIFE happens. Life is there for the taking. Do not judge the 'why and wherefores', for God holds each of you in his hands. But sometimes, we don't listen. We choose to slip through his fingers.

13

The story I now relate begins in a time of plenty when all the Earth was rich in blessings. The day my story begins was just another ordinary day, perhaps like this one but as yet, just another ordinary day.

The sun was high in the sky, as it is this day. Many blessings were being bestowed on the Earth's people. They took all this bounty for granted, not knowing or caring where it came from. Just as little children take the care of their parents for granted, so did my people.

This went on for some time but the day came when I sought to teach them a lesson in gratitude: no more sun, no more rain, no more bountiful harvest.

Dear children, be aware of the forces of evil, of destruction. All cannot continue as it is, for the warnings are there for all to see. Be vigilant. Be aware, for the life you once knew cannot and will not continue. Heed the warning. The control is in your hands. Little by little, I see you destroy all I have given you.

The reason why trees were planted was not only for shelter. It was to help you breathe. The reason why I gave you arms – strong arms – was to give help to your neighbour. The reason why I gave you power over all creatures was so that you could care for them. Do not harm or destroy all my gifts, for they are your 'Life Blood' I created with love. You destroy with greed.

My children, my beloved children, do not turn your back on me, for to do so is to turn your face away from the sun.

But all is not doom. We still have time. I say we,

for are we not partners? Are we not allies? We can if we so choose to, select such a different path.

Look into your hearts. Look beyond the now. We do have a tomorrow. If only we could see past the greed and cruelty.

I am not a revengeful God. I see only that my beloved children have lost their way. Come, come this moment, come and realise that perhaps even you, my dear reader, in your small way and everyday thinking, can arrest this balance.

Do not leave it for your next-door neighbour to be the one. For you, yes, you are someone's next-door neighbour. The burden is yours, not his.

Believe in your instincts. Believe in your goodness. See that you and your neighbour join forces to preserve this land. For much is given to you, much is taken for granted. Be watchful of your neighbour and remind him where he is lacking.

To redress the balance, to right the wrongs of mankind, should be a loving duty. For is not the Father worthy of such loyalty?

My children, I say this with the love of a father who cares for the welfare of all his children, whether animal or human. Does it not seem strange to you that I may seem a vengeful father, a proud father who maybe should let his family perish at their own hands?

But why should all I have created be destroyed by the wants of greedy men?

It is with LOVE that I warn you. It is with compassion that I believe there is deep down in your soul the realisation for the tide to be turned.

So go, my children, and be a brave 'Canute'. Only this time, you can and will succeed in turning the oncoming tide.

14

It should have been a day of great rejoicing. The signs were all there, but she had not and would not listen to all the advice given. Her pride knew no bounds. She knew it all or thought she did.

'What do grown-ups know of such things?' she thought. 'They are past it! Life has passed them by. They are 'has-beens'. Determined to prove to all and sundry that youth in all its glory was the champion of the cause.

The day wore on, and it was not getting any better. Doom and gloom surrounded her, but she knew she was not alone. She had good mates and loyal friends who would stand by her. But where were they now? They should have been here by now. They had promised.

The room was getting dark now. Outside, lights lit up the room, and shadows began appearing. Fear began to grip her, and doubts flooded in.

Was she right? Was this the best decision she had made?

'Too late now,' she thought, 'the forms have been signed, the theatre was ready'. At that, her mind flashed back to another era when all was sweetness and light. Oh, to go back there to that time!

The door opened, and in walked the nurse.

'Are you ready, dear? We are waiting on your final decision.' 'Final?' Yes, it's final. The final time that she would ever contemplate being a 'mother'.

From somewhere in her psyche, a gush of panic gripped her. 'Final, final.' The word echoed around the room. She and only she knew that from this moment on, everything would change.

'But change is good. It's good', she thought.

'Change is a release, as death is a release.' She and only she had the power over the death of this baby.

Death sometimes is good. Death is decay when all usefulness has vanished. What use would a baby be to her? She who was the independent 'Miss.'

But who was she independent of? Her mother, her dad, her teacher? If they were obsolete in her life, why were they there? She had no need of them. But she thought, 'Do they have a need of me?'

Quick as a flash, it hit her. They have a need of me. So why do I care about the pain rising from my stomach? Who needs who in this life? Loneliness was never an option.

When it was all over, when the pain stopped, when the realisation hit her, who now needed her?

(She had a need to need herself. For when one loves, one has a need.)

15

She wandered down the road with a song in her heart. This was going to be a good day. The times of yesterday had passed. Full of glee, the joy of living rose in her, and a song of love and joy filled her being.

'All is well in my world. I am truly blessed,' she thought.

It had been a long struggle, bravely borne. The illness that once invaded her body had gone. She had been one of the lucky ones. The odds of her recovery had been small, but with faith and prayers she had come through this terrible time.

'What of the others?' She thought. 'What of those other unfortunate people who did not make it? That was life, I guess. That is the lottery of life. Some win, some lose.'

But why her? Why had she been singled out to survive? Perhaps in the goodness of time, the reason will be revealed. Her day continued on a wave of bliss and contentment until a strange and unexpected event happened.

Just as she was about to cross the road, a car came whizzing around the corner so fast that it did not see this elderly lady about to cross the road.

Too late, someone screamed. The noise, the thud, it was all over. Then there was silence. A hush descended on this small town.

A lonely bell tolled. It was her day, her long day. Friends gathered to pay their respects. Why they wondered, had this happened? For had she not come through a trial with her illness just to be taken so suddenly?

Is not the time our time? Who owns time? Does life not seem like an endless stream of time? Time to be filled, time to be wasted. Time is elusive. Time streaks on for eternity, but time is not ours. Time is a blessing given to us.

To 'waste time' is a sin. To waste this precious life force, this God-given breath of life, is our undoing. Be constantly alert. Be aware that we do not have tomorrow. Be not glib about 'all the time in the world', for perhaps tomorrow never comes, and you have no time in this world.

16

'How do I compare thee to a rose?' Would it not smell as sweet if given another name? This, she thought, was a wonderful statement.

What is in a name? Is it just a recognisable sound? Is it like a bell, the note that denotes a recognisable tone? How goes the sound of your name? Does it please or grate? Is it a welcoming sound or a grating on your nerves?

The sounds of the world are a cacophony of vibes that echo around the brain, telling us and giving us many messages. Some we listen to, and some we ignore. Why do we pick and choose? Is it because our lives are so busy? Is it because bothering to acknowledge each and every one is just too big an issue? How do we select from 'this and that?' Will we get through our lives any easier by blotting out all the demands that are made to us? Selecting the 'wheat from the chaff' is what we hope to achieve, but, Dear Hearts, how do we know which is which?

Should our fellow man take all our priorities? Should spouses and siblings overrule our demands? Where are we in all of this? Take time for yourself, and heed that little voice that cries for attention. Be not lost in the desert of your desiring. Find that oasis that your soul reaches for. To honour your life force is your just reward.

Be not overwhelmed or guilty by your daydreaming. Your long-awaited dreams take on a reality when in such a blissful state. For is that not just a reward for all the work you have given to others?

Go now and dream! Dream your wildest dreams. Perhaps one day, they will come true. Who knows?

To have a dream is to have hope. To have hope is to be alive. For in wishing on a star, many dreams are fulfilled. For does not your Father listen to all the dreams of his children?

So go and dream your dreams with hope in your heart, for you do not walk alone.

17

Today, she thought, was the beginning of the rest of her life. What more did she need? She had her family now. This was going to be the beginning of a new life. The old one seemed a million miles away.

She was one of the lucky ones. Her life had been turned around at the chance meeting of an old friend. Someone who, down the annals of time, had popped in and out of her life, as do some acquaintances.

She had met her friend out shopping, and just by chance, they came across each other. During their conversation, the topic of their respective families arose. Her friend was a member of a singles club, now having lost her partner. The coincidence of their similarities moved her with compassion.

'How strange,' she thought. 'Both of us share a common situation.'

'Come join me on a Tuesday night. We have fun, and seeing a familiar face there would be nice.' She took the details, said she would consider it, and then they parted.

Did she need to fill her life with a new partner? She thought. She was just beginning to cope on her own. Loneliness was a situation that she had now accepted.

Days passed. Her busy life continued until friends cancelled their plans, leaving her free. Maybe she would go, maybe not. Courage failed her. The thought of new faces eyeing her up and down. 'That's not for me.' No, she would not go. But how many other lonely souls are out there? People like her, who go through life on automatic pilot?

What had she to lose? She could leave if things got uncomfortable. So, putting on her best dress and glamming herself up, she went.

It was not long before the evening took a turn from being sorely uncomfortable to a pleasant surprise, for in through the door walked a familiar face. But yet, no name came to her mind. She was sure she knew him, but where from? Somewhere deep in the depths of her mind, she knew him. She knew this guy.

Pretending not to notice him, she turned to walk away, but he called her name. She stopped in her tracks, turned and smiled. Of course, it is? But no, the name was not obvious. Something disturbed her, a face with no name. Is it better to know a name with no face?

But she recognised that smile – she knew that smile – but where from? All her life, she had been searching for that smile, and he was here, standing before her.

Is not your Father standing before you smiling? Do you not recognise him? You know his name. Maybe you have not seen his face, but he is there. Just turn around, for he is there smiling at you, waiting to be part of your family.

18

'Hold tight,' said the driver, 'we're going round a bend.' As we did, the car swerved, narrowly missing a dog. In his haste to get home, we were all bounced and shaken around.

Home! It sounded good. I had been away from home for a long time. Work and commitments had seen fit to keep me from all I love.

My journeying had taken me to far-flung corners of the Earth, but now that my work was done, I was going home. My heart ached with all that I had missed. All the time of being disconnected from those I loved the most. Not long now until I'd be back in the arms of my family.

My journeying had been a choice of my own making. Not one that I had regretted, but I was tired. My journeyings were all done.

We turned the corner, and there waiting for me was all the family, each one smiling and waving. They had missed me, and I realised how much I had missed them.

When our greetings were over, and all the tears had been shed, I realised this was where I had longed to be all these years. No more to roam and seek the pleasures that cost me dearly. To rest in this glorious place! What more could a heart need?

You, too, are journeying home. How is the journey going? Are you in a dry arid place or where the sun always shines? The choice is yours.

Circumstances may be unavoidable, but do not let your feet dally too long before the climb up your mountain to reach over into the next valley. When there, rest, get your breath and collect your thoughts on the lessons you have learnt before plodding on. The road may be long and twisty, but the road is wide enough for two people.

Have you now realised that though it may seem a long and lonely path, you are not permitted to be alone? Each of us have a guide. Some say an angel, and some believe our ancestors travel with us. But be assured that whoever you believe is with you, you are guided all the way home.

'But where is home?' I hear you say.

Home is where the heart is. Home is where you belong. Home, your home, is being prepared for you. It is your entitlement, whether a palace, mansion or a 'lean-to'. It is not in the deserving. It is not in the reward. It is in the most comfortable place that is right for you.

Do not judge another. Seek not to compare, for your soul knows where the heart longs to rest.

To grow and become that bright shining star that you are only takes time and not much effort on your part but a great deal of patience with your ego.

19

'It's dark in here. It's very dark in here, but it's warm,' she thought.

The only sound to be heard was the slow rhythmic beat of an echo in the distance. The sound was comforting, for she knew this was her connection to the bigger picture in her life.

How long would she be here, wrapped in this cocoon of warm liquid? Many thoughts passed through her mind. Where would she end up when her growing time had passed? What country would be her birthplace? Would she like the family she had chosen? Would they like her? Why had she left home, the place where she knew and the friends she had made?

Curiosity had got the better of her. Tales had been told about a new world, the like of which she had never experienced. Demands were put on her, and a need was requested of her, but the final choice was hers.

Jesus, her beloved angel, had come to her with a request, a need had arisen, and only she could fulfil it.

She was to consider joining a family on the Earth plane. She had never had to make a decision as big as this before. Her life had been one of learning – music, friendship, and tranquillity had filled her days.

Her mission was to go and seek the truth that LOVE is all. The meaning of LOVE was to be her learning.

It seemed a simple task, for she knew about love and felt love and knew that love was being returned to her. But now, cut off from the source, here in this alien world, she was not so sure.

What had she done? She was not so brave now. It was too late to go back. The decision had been made.

She remembered the comforting words spoken to her as she left her other world. 'Remember, you are never alone. You only have to ask for help, for guidance, and it will be given to you.'

She needed help now. Where were the comforting arms? Where were the reassuring arms and smiles?

Her world shook. A mighty force sent her, stretched her, and pushed her through into an opening. She could see a light and hear voices. Warm hands clasped her, and she fell into her new world.

'I have arrived,' she thought, 'now my adventure begins.'

20

Around the corner she came, full of love and blessings for her fellow man.

'Life is good! Life is fine', she thought. 'Nothing can touch me. I feel invincible.'

How is your day? Is your life full of light, full of sunshine? Why should hers be so and not yours?

Does this depend on what side of the bed you got out of? Does it depend on your health or if the sun is shining?

Love comes to us in many ways, least of all through outside interference.

Is love just a state of mind? Do we, at times, look at this world through rose-coloured glasses? Is not the Father watching out for you?

They say 'ignorance is bliss' but who or why does the sun shine for only a few? Are they so blessed with a childlike optimism that reality rarely touches them?

Look to the children. They are our models. See life through their eyes. Grown-ups presume that they are the teacher but consider that maybe children are our teachers when it comes to knowing happiness in their innocence.

Consider a balloon, an ordinary inflated balloon. Give it to a child and what happens? Laughter-filled days, delight lights up their eyes, instant pleasure.

To be in that moment, to realise that we have only that moment, to bring all we have to that moment, to see beauty in the moment – then we are truly blessed.

Go. Live each moment as if it were your last.

21

Have you ever wondered why the grass is green? Why are flowers so colourful? Why are trees so tall? Perhaps not, but please think about this. Let your imagination go wild. Try to see another dimension. We in this 'other world' would like to share something of our world.

To have a belief system, a state of order, is it by chance? It has all been worked out by the divine plan of co-existence.

'Why do birds fly?' You may ask. 'Why do all furry things have four legs?'

Order in all things is not mere chance. Order has been brought out of chaos. The Father of all things has seen fit to bring to you an order so profound that it has become the norm.

You in your world, in your small corner of this vast universe, do not see or understand the logic, the magic, the great scheme that through the annals of time have borne witness to the fruitful co-existence of man and beast.

With great sadness, we see the cruelty and indifference of man's disregard for life. (It's just a dog, it's just a bird, and it's of little importance.) This we see as a belief of many of your fellow men. How little do you know? How little do you care that they are part of you? They are there for a reason.

In the ecology of the human race, nothing is by chance. Everything that has been put on this Earth is for a reason. Do not try to understand *the why* that they are there. In the scheme of things, the knowing is not for you to know. It just IS.

So dear brothers and sisters, the next time you

choose to harm even a fly, even a creepy crawly, think before you stamp on it. For when you do, you are harming yourself. For is it not your belief system 'do unto others as you would have them do to you?' Just because you can, should you?

22

'As of ancient time, man of old did a guiding star behold.' So the carol goes.

Where is your guiding star? Can you see it? Is it visible in your mind's eye? Or is it lost behind a dark cloud?

Do you think you even need a guiding star? Are you of a mind that 'no one is going to lead me to a place not of my choosing?' Does this thought ever cross your mind?

'Where am I going in my life? What has life got to offer me? Am I making the right choices?' For you have many decisions to make.

Is it just a coincidence when we meet and marry our lifelong partners? Who decides how many children, or even if children are to be born to you? Is it really your decision? And why do people come and then suddenly, for no real reason, leave your life?

Think about the stages within your life. Your youth and then how you matured into adulthood. The slow pace of old age. It is all the natural progress of a guiding hand.

To each of us, this is the norm. It is a pattern we expect to follow, but sometimes fate takes a hand, and the norm is no more.

Where is your 'star' then? Has its light gone out? Has it evaporated into thin air?

He who guides your 'star' (whether you believe it or not) guides you as a father guides his young children, for each of us follows the same pattern. But beware of the self-assurance that even though life to you may seem all a lottery, all coincidences and all choices are not of your making. Look to the times when in your daily life problems have arisen. Where was your 'star' then? Did you look to your 'star' for guidance? Or did you think that you could solve the problems on your own?

Be assured that your 'star' is shining for you. See and believe, for the guidance is there. Hold onto that 'star', for it will see you through many dark days until it leads you home.

Trust your 'star' for it knows the way.

23

It is said, 'He that believeth in me, yet he be dead shall gain glory in heaven.' A contradiction, you may say, to be dead is to be dead.

So how can he be alive in heaven? To be dead in the logical sense is to be void of all life. The saints may tell us of glory yet unseen, but how do we on the Earth plane understand such a statement?

Go back in time and remember a situation when your logical brain ruled over you. The access you had then was of such basic reasoning that all seemed doom and gloom. To struggle was the norm. It takes a crisis of faith, a crisis in your health, to awaken a deeper sense of the 'alternative'. But what is the 'alternative', you may ask? To see the other side of the coin, to seek deep beneath the surface of the 'other side of life', a layer you have forgotten ever existed.

They say, 'Hope springs eternal', but what is hope? Just a glorified branch, a helping hand of some forgotten benefactor that left you long ago down the annals of time when you were young and feeling brave?

Are you so blinkered? Do you not see what is there before you? Do you even want to see a better day? Would it hurt your eyes too much to see the sunshine?

Go beyond your logical reasoning. 'Wake up and smell the roses,' I cry. Wake up to the belief that what you have been given is only just the burden of that day. It is up to you to judge it, to deal with it in the only way you know how. But that is the crux. That is when those who see the 'other side of the coin' get through their day with ease.

There is another side to life. Have patience and

have an awareness that things will get better. That you are not alone. That the darkness is your enemy and that you are your own worst enemy.

The 'fear' is your enemy. Fear of the unknown is such a weight that you place around your neck. Release it, let it go, let it drop from your shoulders.

For fear is your enemy, fear is your darkness. Release it, let the sunshine in, lose that frown and see the light begin to shine in your eyes. Believe in rainbows. Believe that your tomorrows can only get better.

For when you do that, you are truly awake. For why travel on a rough and stony highway when you can glide along a smooth and shiny surface?

24

'He that is born of man, though he be as a small child, yet shall he enter the kingdom of heaven.' Is that our just reward? Is that taken for granted?

Dear Hearts, open your eyes, see and speak of the wonders of the Lord.

Do you not know that your kindly Father waits to be asked into your life? See and believe in the force that awaits your beckoning. Do not be troubled with mundane, with trivia. Gossip is just an idle pastime. It demeans your character. Choose a higher level of vibration. Choose to be as an angel would see the world.

Do I ask you to aim too high? Why are you not there already? Is your lowly world so wonderful, immense, and full of gold, wonder and blessings that peace and tranquillity fill your very being?

I think not – but it can be and could be. You have a choice. Believe you have a choice. It is not just for the saints of this world. It could be the norm of this world.

Why not give it a try? What have you to lose? For you have much to gain. Your heart has a longing. Do you not get a glimpse of it in a flower, in the setting of your sun, in a child's happy face? Turn and face that day. Turn and face a new tomorrow. You have a choice. Take that choice, turn and see. Open those veiled eyes, and let the darkness slip away, for no one really wants cloudy, dark, cold days. See the light – the light that is there. It begins as a pinpoint. For as you open up to let more of the light in, see it whoosh and fill your day until you become part of that light. Until you *become* the light.

So go and shine your light. Light up someone else's world. Show them how to become a spark until this 'infection' spreads throughout your world.

Are you prepared to become 'infected'? To live and share your 'infection'?

This is one ailment that the Lord will find no cure for.

25

Are you happy this day? Does life skip by you with a feeling of bliss?

'Nonsense!' I hear you cry. 'Life is but one big struggle. One big battle of wits between me and the next man. 'It was a sunny morning, just an ordinary day like this one.

She walked along the road, trying to block out the sounds of the traffic and the sound, the grating sound of her troubles. For it had been on a day just like this when the accident happened. Her mind flashed back to that awful day.

It had begun as an ordinary family day out. Lots of preparation, sandwiches to be made, bucket and spade to be found, dog to be calmed and coaxed.

What had been planned was a day at the seaside, but that day in all its expectation did not materialise. Tragedy struck on the approach road to the beach.

The sun was bright that day, blue sky and little cloud, perfect, or so they thought.

No one knows exactly what happened. It happened so quickly. Where the lorry came from, or why it should have been on that particular road, no one knew.

Her mind skipped the rest. The horror lay buried deep down. It was too painful to go there.

She continued her walk, alone in her 'might have beens'. 'But this,' she thought, 'will get me nowhere. I must move on and make a fresh start. But it's lonely here on my own.' To grasp each branch that is given to us, to see through different eyes the possibilities of a new existence is all that she could hope for.

For help, she knew, was there. It had taken a

long time to realise that she had to ask first. For help will come, help is always there. We just have to remember to ask for it.

For your Father knows what you carry. He sees you struggle. He waits to help, and he waits to be needed in your struggle.

Go and ask, go and share all your burdens, for is he not your Father? A loving, doting Father who longs to be of service? Why struggle so when the mighty hand of God waits to carry you?

26

It is said, 'He that is born of man though he be of lowly birth yet shall he attain great heights.'

Is this something you believe in? Is it just for the 'great and the good'?

Where do you see yourself fitting into this fable?

The populace would have us believe that man is as insignificant as a grain of sand. To ever think that he can rise above his station in life is indeed dabbling with delusion.

Is man born with this inability to disown his worth, to see himself as anything less than ordinary?

'Pride', they say, 'goes before a fall'. Who decides on these sayings? Parables are written by cynics.

Does not he of good stature ever contemplate the laws of natural justice? That even he who cast the first stone is blameless.

The Father sees in each of you a being of such immense possibilities. If only we look to Him and see the potential of our being.

We cannot all be Einstein. We all cannot put our names to some wonder drug that can save mankind, but all we can be is the best that we can be. The best at listening to a friend, the best at making a cup of tea for the homeless, the best at giving up our spare time for a worthy cause.

We cannot all reach great heights and gain recognition through awards in the press. But what we can do, is all we can do.

The world needs you, so play your part. Small is BIG in the eyes of the Lord.

27

It fell upon a summer's day that as she was painting her house, a butterfly landed on her newly painted windowsill.

'Bother,' she said. 'Go away. You spoil my work.' As swift as it came, it went.

Replenishing her brush, she went over the bleb. The sun dried her paintwork, and no blemishes were to be seen.

How often do we hide our blemishes and mistakes with a fresh coating of disbelief, pretence, and denial?

Do we allow the cover-up to be seen by others, or simply ignore what is blatantly obvious?

Are we, as little children then, pretending in our games? Do we, like the butterfly, flit from one mistake to the next with complete disregard for others?

When our mistakes are shown to us, and our consciences prevail, do we try our bluff?

Be as the butterfly – tread lightly in daily doings. The Father knows and sees all the cover-ups, the mistakes, for you see the error of your ways only when your imprint has been noted. For what is he, who in seeing his mistakes, makes amends to obliterate the bleb with a fresh coat of determination of belief and goodwill?

There is a saying, 'Be careful where you tread in the snow. Your footprints will show.'

28

Let's talk about friendships.

What would we do without our beloved friends? Who would send us flowers when we are ill? Who would be there with a cup of tea when problems need discussing? A friend is our 'earth angel' who takes delight in our company, who loves us 'warts and all'.

To have a friend is indeed to be blessed. Can you imagine your life without your best friend? What pain that would cause you. Treat your friend as you would your prize possession, for they are indeed beyond the price of any pearl.

You have many friends, seen and unseen, some who walk beside you, some that you cannot see, yet they are there. Those who never leave your side do not mind being ignored, but how much more joyous would your life be if you shared your joys and problems with them? Some call them angels, and some call them guides, but what is in a name? Call them 'special', for indeed they are, for they are the ones who work those little miracles that you know could never have happened without their intervention. So, remember now and again to bless your unseen friends, for they are mighty and more constant, more forgiving than any 'earth angel'.

29

It fell upon a summer's day as Mary Jane was walking down the lane, not a care in the world. To her, this day was a blessing, for she had come far in her development. Her mind and body were of purer essence now. Not like before in her grief, when her world was one of coldness and dejection, of such dark emptiness that life, her so-called life, barely existed. She shuddered at the remembrance of this.

But all this was now a distant memory – never to go down that road again – for she had turned the corner.

On her travels this day, she came upon the crossroads in the bend of her well-trodden path into town. She hesitated. Someone blocked her way. Not a visible barrier, though it felt visible. An unseen brick wall had now been placed before her. Puzzled, her mind spinning for an explanation, she tried to move forward, but her way was blocked. What to do? She smiled a wry and knowing smile.

Is life like this? The decisions we make when we come to a crossroads in our lives. Does it all depend on which road we take, which turning we take, the choices we all make in our lives – where we end up?

In the bigger scheme of things, do we, in our innocence, have a choice? Perhaps choices are made for us. It is so easy to be wise after the event, but until then, we are at the mercy of our own truths.

The decision can be of our making, but perhaps there is an unseen force that, once tapped into, can help us decide the right road and decisions in our choices.

Do we stop to consider that we even have a

choice? Do we think that whatever I choose is my choice? Consider this, then, why do we have a left and right brain, logic and fantasy? Does making any decision, big or small, take into consideration the outcome of that choice?

When things go awry over a bad choice, who is to blame? Do we look inward at ourselves? Do we blame others or see the lesson we need to learn?

All choices in our lives are there as a test for us, a test in our progress on life's pathway, to move on, to improve our well-being and stature.

Some decisions are hard. We would prefer never to have to make some of our decisions. But what is life? What has our zest for life been if we do not take that first tentative step forward?

For man is here to learn by making the 'wrong turning', the 'wrong decision'. Do not be fooled into believing that life has to be sweetness and rosy for you. By making difficult decisions, grow and expand your consciousness. That moves you into ever-increasing glory.

So go for it and make your decisions in your life. See beyond the next bend in the road, for life is for the living.

Be like Mary Jane. Slow down and consider which turning you make, but remember that in making a choice, logic may not prevail. But it is in the deciding that we are truly alive.

30

As the sun began setting over the hills, its glow filled the sky. Already the night star began its nightly watch. She sighed. It has been a good day. It had been a very good day overall. She could not believe the continuousness of events that had taken place a few hours previously.

Her mind jumped back a few hours. The realisation that a plan, a series of events, a play that seemed to have needed to be acted out had taken place around her.

'Are we merely puppets in someone's grand plan of things?' she thought. 'Where is the puppet master in all of this?'

For her, it felt like some unseen hands were working behind the scenes. Her troublesome son, the bane of her life, was yet again in bother with the law. She had tried to bridge the gap between them until she had eventually given up on him.

What was she to do? His rebellious attitude had seen him deteriorate into this stranger who was no longer part of her, the boy she once loved and knew.

Other people, other forces had seen fit to take over his life. She missed him. Oh, how she had missed him when he moved out of her house.

'He needed to breathe', he had said, 'to live life to the full.' For him, life was there for the taking, at whatever cost. The years passed, and she saw and heard little of him. What she did hear was not good.

But fate, in its wisdom, had seen fit to take a turn, and events so amazing began happening. Newspaper reports spread of a local man. They reached her ears, but still nothing concrete as to who this amazing lad was. It seems that this young lad had saved a trapped animal and put his own life in danger. A worthy cause indeed, but hardly likely to be her Charlie. Charlie, who had hatred and a cruel streak for tormenting such innocent creatures.

Time passed, and she heard no more. Rumours began again. This time a name and a photo appeared in the local paper. It was her Charlie, but how different he appeared – neat haircut, neatly shaven beard, and no rips in his clothes! But how? Or even why? It confused her. Where had he been? How had his life changed so much? A hero, once more?

Events took a different turn, and she became ill. Having tried to find her son and failed, she believed that her life had failed too.

But who are we in the bigger picture of life not to see that life itself must be played out? Each scene and each line have to be noted and acted upon.

The puppet master is all in this. He sees the players acting their part and brings the play to its final curtain call. But please let me remind you that the characters, the playing out of each part on the earth stage, is in the choices we each make.

To be the villain, the heroine or the evil witch is our choice.

So play your part in this wonderful theatre of life. But remember you choose which character you play.

31

The sages old did little but spout profound and earth-shattering pearls of wisdom. What else did they do with their time? This is a question, a puzzlement to me.

Have you pondered that these wise men of old – and why have only men been recorded? – sat on some grassy bank in the sun, being waited on hand and foot?

Who cooked for them, fed them, shopped for them, and cleaned their clothes? I could go on.

Were they ever married? Did they have children? I suspect not. Their minds were on higher things.

To the average person walking the streets, their world is a world of sunny climes, where the sun always shines, and blue seas lap the shore. Not in cold old England, beautiful though she is. But warm and deep, profound thoughts always seem to go together.

But to exist in this world there has to be contrast, for how do we know good if we do not know evil? Rest awhile and think of other similes. To know and appreciate happiness, joy and bliss, we must know sorrow, fear and rejection. Our world is indeed a world of contrast – a beautiful and frightening contrast.

As we travel through life, the appreciation of this thought sees us through many a trial. To come out of this, to come out of any situation as though coming through a dark tunnel into the light, the trial, the lesson is over. It is then that our soul soars onto a different level.

We who see ourselves as mundane, average, not so special, the busy ants of this world, more a doer than a thinker – there lies the contrast. Someone had to wash their clothes, cook their meals, and clean up after them. So do not decry your job, your life, or your situation.

The wheels that turn industries begin at the top with the managing director and the money people, all the way down to the guy who sweeps up and makes the tea.

Do not, in your despair, decry your worthlessness. The worth that the Lord places in you is far beyond the measure you place in yourself, for I am sure that the so-called 'managing director' would sometimes (on his bad days) willingly swap places with the guy who sweeps up and makes the tea.

So, go and shine, for who knows who longs to change places with you.

32

How come you think this day has been given to you as the worth that you deserve? Is it not a mere chance that perhaps some God, some deity, saw to give you another chance? In doing so, the trial begins all over again.

'The days of our years are numbered', or so we are told. Perhaps you have lived long already. Perhaps you are just a youth, young and fresh on the brink of your life.

Whatever, wherever you are in whatever span of this life you now exist, stop for a moment and set aside mundane things. Step into that beam of light, of suspension, to look around you. Being so detached as if you have disappeared from all conscious realms and see. Look and see where you are in your life.

Do you even like your life? Do the people in your life like you, resemble you or connect with you? Are you seeing what is real or what you hope and imagine to be real? Is life to you a challenge, a battle, a job so hard that there are days when you wonder, 'How long can I go on doing this?'

People may seem uncaring. Being taken for granted is the norm. 'Would they miss me if I was not here? They would be sorry then, too late!' Would be the cry.

Why waste this precious gift, the gift we all take for granted? The role that you are playing out is simply your survival technique.

The path you tread may have been laid for you. It may have been the one you choose to walk. Not to your liking? Then choose a different path.

'But there are obstacles in the way!' I hear you

shout. Are there? Are they there of our making or of what life has seen fit to place before us? Is there no way around these obstacles? Do we choose for them to remain so that the choices, the excuses we give, are taken from us?

Look deep and ponder on that thought.

To escape. To be brave. Is that what we really want, or is it so cosy and natural to continue in the same vein, never having the courage to do anything other than lay the blame at other people's door?

You choose. Are you brave enough for change? Are you willing to step out of the 'norm' to be who you truly are, not the mechanical person others expect you to be? It may take time. You may never succeed, for others may rebel and try to control you, chipping away at your confidence just at the vital time of victory.

Why deny your heart? How does your soul ever sing its song? You owe your life to no one. You were born to be glorious. The choice, whether right or wrong, choices are merely stepping stones on our journey through life. Do not be burdened or downtrodden with responsibilities. You can jump from one to the other. Never resting long on each stone.

Think on this when you come back from your dreaming. The sun is there for you as well as others.

For the Son knows what you long for. Ask him to show you the way. He waits on your call.

Do not leave it too long, for in seeking help, you step into the light, a light that never goes out.

33

Today may be the day when all your dreams come true. A wish, a dream, for without dreams, where would we be?

'To dream the impossible dream, to fight the unbeatable foe', goes the song. And yet, just maybe the dream, that wonderful reoccurring dream, may come true. If only we wish hard enough or are good enough, it may come true.

What do you dream of? Wealth, happiness, good health, or enough money to sail away to some distant shore? 'If only', you cry, 'if only'.

They are truly blessed in the animal kingdom with a sense of realisation that they have the dream now. Humans, in their wisdom, go one better, always seeking what they do not possess.

'Nothing wrong in that', I hear you say. Nothing indeed, but contentment, having more than your just desserts is the quest.

The humble sparrow goes about his daily 'doings' – not for him the glorious terrain of mountain peaks, for he knows his place in the order of creation.

The little Jenny wren, sweet and dainty, a tiny creature blessed with a sweet voice, is just as happy in her life as the majestic peacock in all his finery.

So where do you see your place in life?

Is just being who you are not enough? Then go and seek your pot of gold at the end of the rainbow. But perhaps you are already there, and you don't know it.

For is the grass really a better shade of green over that hill?

Does the sun really shine brighter over there?

Go and seek if you must but remember what you leave behind.

34

As she sat beneath her favourite tree, lost in her make-believe world, dreaming of events yet to happen, she suddenly realised that all her life, well at least for many months, this had been the pattern of her idleness.

And yet to be idle was not a bad thing, not a wasted thing. To dream afar and see beyond her daily drudge was all that kept her sane.

Her tree, her friend, knew of her dreams, but no one else did, for she had no one to confide in.

Her tree was splendid. It shaded her from the sun in the summer and kept her dry from the rain. Her tree was something she could rely on. It was always there and never let her down. It was strong and dependable.

She talked to her tree like a friend, for that is how she saw it. We all need a friend, be they human or not. The sounds we make when we vocalise our wishes, whether large or small, bring that reality from the subconscious into the conscious. From there, into a reality that the ethos can make happen. For action follows thought.

Do you have a dream? Speak it. Tell a friend. Go tell your favourite tree.

For in doing so, the universe, in its wisdom, may grant your dream. For who knows where the trail ends?

Sound is a powerful source of energy. So shout it out loud from the mountaintops where your greatest friend can hear you, for a whisper keeps it a secret.

35

Today it is raining. 'Into every heart, some rain must fall', goes the song. It is only temporary. The sun always shines after the rain.

But today, it is a black, gloomy day when the clouds, nay all heaven, seems to be at its darkest. She thought on this. She pondered what would happen, supposing the sun never shone again.

Oh dear, what a bleak thought! Never to have flowers growing, no more picnics in the country, days lazing on the beach. She dismissed the thought as quickly as it came.

But ponder a moment. Take stock of this thought! And your assumptions are?

We take so much for granted, do we not? But who is it that sees? Who decides when the rain must fall or when the sun shines?

Are we so small, so childlike in our assumptions that all is being taken care of? Balance is everything. Balance is a force of nature.

See your world as a fine line between two worlds, for sorrow and pain, happiness and smiles are just a thought away.

'Too deep, too profound, too many 'what ifs?'', I hear you complain.

Think on and believe that just maybe, if you live each moment as if that is all you have, then the possibilities can come true.

We all have good days. We all have bad days. This we accept. So why does man grumble when the rain falls or when bleak and dissolute happenings occur? To know one, one must know and appreciate the other. Have your moments of doubt and despair, but see through them as temporary, for much more awaits you when the darkness passes. Be as the animals, have your 'wintertime' of darkness, loss, and frugal pleasures.

But when that first ray of sun brightens up your sky – because she knows, for she is in perfect balance with nature – be as the dove when it first saw land. Fly to reach that first ray of light and know that life is being redressed. Now all is well, and your living can begin again.

For does not the snowdrop know when to push through the dark soil to let all know that we are still alive and that the roses will bloom soon?

36

To be a 'star' to shine for all to see! Would you like to be a star?

A TV star? A star in your class at school or college? A star with your family and friends? Perhaps you are, and you don't know it.

Do you ever wonder why stars exist at all? Stars that shine so on dark frosty nights. Ever wondered about star formations, the Bear, Orion's belt, the Plough etc.? Who made the stars, and why?

Go back to when you were small, so small you were yet to be conceived. Do you remember when the first spark of life suddenly jerked you into existence? For you, time had begun.

In saying this, I draw to illustrate the beginning of time. Each of us has a 'time', an existence, a life span of our own, just as the world has a life span of its own.

Never doubt this, my friend, in being so entrenched in your ways that you believe you are invincible, for each of us rides a different course. For the Lord is the giver of life. He sees fit when life is no more.

The length of time we have on this Earth plane is not a lottery and has nothing to do with being in the wrong place at the wrong time, but it is his and only his decision.

The 'good' do not die young, and no one gets his 'just reward', for man foolishly explains all shortening of life thus. Be grateful to the Lord for your life, for it is a gift that man takes so lightly.

Just as the stars (for they do have a life span) die and fade away, we too do when your life span is over.

But what remains? Only the memory, only the impression of what we have left behind? I think not. We leave much behind – friends and family. Our imprint on this world will then be the better for it. For as you travel on your pathway, stop and look up at the stars, see and wonder at them. See how they twinkle and glow in the night sky. Do they remind you of anybody, of anything?

Could they be some lost and dead planets, the impression of which now remains?

What impression would you like to leave behind?

Be as the star, twinkle and glow NOW for all to see.

37

A child is born today. Great joy is all around him. He has entered a new world where he will be loved, needed and wanted. A lucky child indeed. Not all children born into this world are needed, wanted or even welcomed. But who is to blame for this sad outcome?

We are told, on the one hand, that all life is a gift from God, yet poverty pervades many countries, and the populations are ever on the increase. So why does God allow babies to be born in these countries?

We all know the biological reason – man's inability to restrict his desires. But in times of famine, there is little or no control.

These dear babies are a blessing on God's Earth. Do you not see that God, in his wisdom, delivers these babies to us as a sign, as proof of his love?

'But babies are dying because of poverty.' I hear you cry. Yes, they are, but do you not see that it is because man, in his greed, sees fit not to share his wealth?

So who is to blame? God on the one hand for procreation, or man in his greed on the other? I see your heart bleeds for these children, but there is a lesson to learn. Greed, in all its ugliness, pervades your psyche, and excuses are many.

The solution? Dig deep into your heart, see and look around at your own beliefs. The solution is there. Love and support these children, for they are part of your world.

The test is, the lesson is, of how and why is our perception of justice, or injustice of man's greed. The souls of these dear children are born and reborn with love and blessings from the Creator. The children are a lesson, a test of our times. This may sound brutal to all sensitive people, even cruel, but man has not learned his lesson yet.

Wealth is a state of mind as well as a big bank balance. The feeling that I have enough, and I am keeping it is about the average thought form. What is 'enough'? No one admits to having too much. But most people, 90% of people, have more than enough for their needs.

It is not about donations. It is not about a monthly sum that is given. It is about our ability to give that part of us, that unseeing part of us, a piece of ourselves, our time, our love, our prayers, and our blessings.

Money could solve the problem, but poverty will always be at our heels until we learn to love our fellow man more than we love ourselves.

Make it a priority. Your priority! Make poverty a thing of the past, a war that can be won if only we give up ourselves.

38

Clouds. Now there is an interesting topic, is it not?

We have fluffy white ones. We have dark black ones. Some are so big that they hide the sun, some so small and wispy that one puff of wind and they disperse. Do you ever wonder about clouds, how they are formed, or why they even exist at all?

We talk of the 'storm clouds gathering' when trouble is brewing, a 'silver lining' around a cloud when troubles are over.

Have you ever laid on the grass and watched the clouds go racing by on warm sunny days? Where do they go? Who will see them after you? What do clouds hide? Are they there as a screen to shade us from the sun? Your imagination could run riot.

Is life for you like that? Just as the clouds rush by us, your life too is all rush. Never stopping to 'smell the roses' on your way.

Next time you notice clouds, be they white and fluffy or dark and heavy with rain, stop and think. Imagine a day when you can step out of your life and go and sit on your cloud. Where would you go? What would you see? Remember, you have no control over your cloud, for unseen hands direct their route.

Imagine. Let your mind wander to unseen places, people, and lands, so removed from your norm that you could be on a different planet.

But you are not. You are here. Resign yourself to the same earth that many others know not of you, but you can get to know them, see them, touch them, care for them, and bless them.

To drift around on your lonely white cloud may sound like bliss, but in reality, to touch Earth, to come down from your cloud is what will make our planet a much better place.

For this is where the living exists. Clouds are meant for dreaming on. Earth is where you live.

So once in a while, step off your cloud and join others in this wonderful time that we have. In doing so, every day is a 'white cloud' day.

39

It all began one sunny morning. Just an ordinary day as today is. Getting out of bed, she drew the curtain to admire the sunshine, the blue sky and the view.

'Nice day,' she thought, 'all is well in my world'.

The day continued. Her life continued. Until about mid-day, when it all turned into a disaster. Little did she know that her world was about to come crashing down.

It was not of her doing, for she was the innocent party, but the forces had seen fit to end her day on a low note.

How she had fought against the ruling, against the tide that now threatened to engulf her. She must be strong. She must not let them see that she was struggling. But sink she did. She could fight no more. Little by little, each wave got stronger and stronger until her strength gave out.

The problem began in a small way. She could cope. She did not need anyone's help. She realised that the stream of water that began as only a trickle suddenly came crashing through her door. She had no time to run, for there was nowhere to run.

The stream at the bottom of her garden had burst its bank and was now a raging torrent of water. Furniture began to float, bobbing about, pieces crashing into each other. There was no escape, for the water was now up to her neck. She was trapped inside this tomb of a house.

It is in times of panic, in times of danger we cry out to the Almighty to save us, for it is human nature to do so. Is the Lord only there for us in times of stress and danger? I think not, for he is always with us, but we forget. Speak to the Lord when your times are good, and life is 'sunshine and joy', for does he not deserve our attention? To only rely on him when danger beckons, is that fair? Is that considerate?

Reverse the situation. For God, in his goodness and mercy, forgives all who lean on him. His shoulders are mighty. But consider this – where does God come into your life when all is 'happy, sunshine and roses?' Do you think he is not here? You have no need of him then? Are you so fickle that you do not see how often God forgives you and how hard it is to be taken for granted? But God is Love. His love knows no end. It is us that pay the price of neglect.

40

As you know or may not know, 'He who seeks knowledge, whether by books, by exploration, or by TV, is so blessed. He who is idleness is less than holy.'

Are you a waster or a seeker? Does your heart long to know the truth, the 'reason why' it happens? Or are you a fool who accepts all that is disclosed to him?

Harsh words indeed, 'straight to the bone'. Is your belief system so contrived that it is so simple that a child has more curiosity than you?

Think about politicians standing on their platforms, pontificating their doctrine. Is it that you have heard it all before? Is it that it takes too much effort for you to be bothered whether it makes sense? That you don't even give them the 'time of day?' Where do you stand in all of this? Does your gut feeling tell you anything? Those who truly believe that 'ignorance is bliss' live in such a cosy warm bubble, blind to the obvious and fast asleep.

'Wake up!' I shout. 'Wake up and smell the roses before it is too late.' The Lord gave you a brain. Use it. And use it so you see what is beneath the surface. Go and seek out the 'alternative'.

How many times do I need to shout out this message? How many generations does it take to wake mankind to see the truth for themselves? Do not leave it to others to make every decision for you. Do not, in your ignorance, follow like sheep. Step out of the crowd, and be your own master, for time will tell who is right. It may sound scary. People may laugh and point the finger, but so what? Who is there to judge you? Be not intimidated. You are a glorious being who stands by his truth. Step out of the herd and let people see you do this, 'by your actions ye are known'.

Courage is yours for the taking. Does it matter what others think of you? At the end of the day, being true to your soul is all that matters. The peace and contentment that comes with this thought form is worth it. Stand up and be counted for your beliefs! Why is that not what the saints of old did? They were glorious in their convictions. Yours may not be so grand, but the victory is still yours.

So, my dear friend, next time a decision has to be made, big or small, think about what I have said. Go with that 'gut' feeling. Does it matter that you contradict the person standing next to you? Knowing that you speak your truth is what the saints of old did. Do not be intimidated by the majority for being different. Stand up and be counted, for the victor of the soul is yours.

41

When you look at a tree, what do you see?

'A tree is a tree', you may say. How does a tree feel? Why do we have trees? Are they merely there to block a view, give us shade and help the ozone layer? Stop and think awhile.

Do you have a favourite tree, a tree that shelters you from the rain and gives you shade in the summer? Or do you even see a tree as a blinking nuisance when they shed their leaves and make a mess, causing you more work in the garden?

But look again at any tree, touch it, feel its texture, smell it, judge its height. Perhaps you even know the name of your favourite tree.

What about the shape of trees? Some are tall and slim, some wide and stubby, some that flower and bear fruit, others only found by the water, and others only in dry areas.

Would you miss trees if, by some quirk of fate, they all died? Be honest now, would you? Perhaps some of you would, some perhaps not.

Ecology has seen fit to give the reason for trees. They are the 'lungs' of the Earth.

But trees are more than that, much more. Norma, in her wisdom, sees trees as 'old men', old and wise beings who have stood the test of time. An analogue of wisdom and knowledge. They have seen battles. They know of droughts, of castles, of the shaping of this world and of history itself.

Next time you see a tree, honour that tree, for that tree is your guardian. It is a testimony of the truth that will not die.

Please love all trees. Bless them. Hug them. Lean on them. They welcome all. None is discriminated against. The mighty force of a tree only seeks to serve man and the animal kingdom. A truth we take for granted.

42

As you know, or may not know, it is written 'that by our actions ye are known.'

How goes that statement with you? Do you care what people think about you? Does it matter that many do not like you? Do you even care what is said about you?

Are you brave enough or blind enough to think that in the bigger scheme of things, people are only there to be made use of?

Many that I see act as if they and they alone have the right, the judgement of Solomon. But I say unto you, 'Judge not another, lest you yourself be judged.'

Perhaps I need to explain myself here. I see much with my mind's eye. I see and smile at all the antics that the human race acts out in their pursuit of happiness.

Dear Hearts, I care that you struggle. I care that your lives are hard and that you feel that just surviving takes all the willpower and tenacity you can drum up. The struggle I see, the independence that you choose to take from me.

Please stop and consider this. You were not meant to struggle on your own. But to step back from a problem, a situation so big that it devours you, leaving you feeling 'that this is too much for me to bear, that I cannot go on'.

Release it, release it and send it to me.

You were not meant to be on your own. You were not meant to live without God. For when you left me, did we not make a pact? Did we not agree that we were together in this life and the next one?

Dear Hearts, do not forget me. I only seek to remind you that love, mutual love, is a force that we share.

Sometimes I see flashes of remembrance. I see and touch. You hear only when you remember me. I go nowhere. I leave you not. I am at your right hand.

My dear children, release your will to a higher authority. Do not let pride devour you in the belief that you have to go it alone. May I gently remind you that in choosing to disobey our agreement, you lose the ability to 'grow in the light'.

Why struggle? Why make living so difficult for yourselves? Life was never meant to be difficult. You came here to learn many lessons, this we agreed. But when the living of it became too much, the lessons were too hard. This was when you released your will to me.

We are in partnership, you and me. I am not a 'sleeping partner'. I am here waiting for you, waiting in my boardroom. Let's discuss the latest crisis. Are two heads not better than one?

43

As Jesus once said, 'He that is heavy laden, come to me, and I will give you rest.'

'There once was an ugly duckling, with feathers all stubby and brown', goes the song. So ugly that no one liked him. In fact, they all laughed at him.

Are you part of that audience? Or are you that duckling? It is not preaching. It's not a reprimand or pointing the finger. It is about being in a situation where you are that person, of being in that person's shoes.

No? Not brave enough, easy to point and scorn, easy to laugh and stare? 'Others do it! So, I can.'

Stop for a moment and stand back and reflect on this. This soul, this being whom you ridicule, is as brave a soul as you will ever meet. The pact that was made before 'it' reincarnated is testimony to its bravery.

Happy endings are few. Sure, the duck turned into a swan for all to see. But what of the scars inside, the ones that we cannot see?

Was the swan a happy swan, a loving and gentle being? Or was its nature to be angry and a bully (because of past treatment?) Cruelty, in all its ignorance, is an abomination. The wounds that are inflicted thus, warp and bend the victim's mind until that person becomes the victim of a sick society. The populace feels and believes that theirs is the right to do so.

Perhaps my story makes you blush, makes you feel a little guilty in remembrance of past deeds? That's OK. That is human nature, which is good.

For in remembering, we learn a great lesson. If feeling guilty, even sorry, that to us is indeed a cleanser.

So remember, could you be that brave? Could you willingly live as a disfigurement, a glaring oddity? Humility, tolerance and patience, are they just words, or are they 'should be's'?

You, perhaps, are one of the lucky ones. Beauty and flow of speech are yours. These are only outward flaws. They do not reflect the inward flaws. So maybe you can now judge who is to blame? Who is it that values the soul, the character of that person?

What is so perfect in your makeup that you can point the finger? Like the swan, beauty on the outside does not guarantee beauty on the inside. Is beauty only skin deep?

44

Are you sitting comfortably? Then I will begin. There once was a little boy, a gentle and sweet-natured child everyone loved and adored. He wanted for nothing. Love, toys and money were his for the asking. Nothing was too much trouble for his parents. They doted on him. Love was all around him. He had everything his heart could desire. Blessed little boy, indeed, his life was one continuous round of blessings.

Then came the day when his parents died. They died in a car crash. He was suddenly alone. By this time, he was ten years old. Life for him was about to take a dramatic turn. Where was he to go? Who was going to look after him now? Aunts and uncles were never on the scene. He never knew any of his extended family.

Then fate took a hand in the next stage of his life. Due to some clause in his parents' will, Samuel was to go and live abroad with a maiden aunt, a lady Samuel never knew existed. Saying his goodbyes to friends and teachers, he set off on his journey. This was scary. Exciting but scary. Having never set foot outside of England, never gone further than the next town, the world to him seemed to become very large indeed.

The flight took ten hours. He had only seen these distant shores in books.

He was greeted very warmly by a rather strict, domineering lady much older than his mother but not old, old. How he had wanted to fling his arms around her, to be greeted by a hug. But it was not to be.

They were in the car, travelling very quickly down a dusty road. People there seemed to walk a lot, all in single file, and this Samuel thought very strange, as it was so hot at this time of day.

Where was he going? How long would it take to get there? These questions ran around his head. He had learned from his parents that one had to wait to be spoken to before he could ask questions.

They were here. They had arrived at his new home. Rushing out to explore his new surroundings, he realised that now his life was to begin anew. Gone were England's cold, dark days, for this country only knew sunlight and blue skies.

He chose not to compare, for what had passed could not be obtained anymore. That was the day Samuel grew up. What he had lost was a life of immeasurable beauty. This was less, but it was all he had. In his realisation that the life that was now his was so far removed, yet another chance had been given to him, and from this, he would grow.

When changes occur in our lives, when all we know is taken from us, to progress and to step out of the norm takes courage. It makes us look to a different horizon. But perhaps 'different' could be better, could mean that the gods have seen fit to move us onto the next stage in our development.

Progress is all. Progress is what our world is about. Do you not see that sometimes when big changes occur, though they can be frightening and you may panic, trust that though they are painful, a bigger picture is waiting for us to see?

So, if life thrusts you out of your warm, cosy nest onto a thin, shaky branch, is that not where the best fruit can be had? For life begins outside your comfort zone.

45

The realisation that God is 'All' is a very profound statement.

It seems that the belief we place in Him as the provider of all is a challenge on the senses. We all need a 'whipping boy' in our lives, someone to blame when things go wrong.

Others may see him as the eternal Father figure, lurking above us, waving the proverbial big finger at us when we go astray.

How does God appear to you? Is it with fear and trepidation? The softly approach, tiptoeing along, hoping he does not notice us. Or as the ever-smiling 'Santa Claus' image, benign and benevolent?

Is he either of these two images, or is he more?

Perhaps in our child-like state, we choose to believe that all is well until we slip and fall out of grace yet again. Saying our 'Hail Marys', promising never to be wicked again, then going merrily on our way.

I say unto you, he that believeth in me, in my laws of justice and mercy shall know better days. His is the glory.

But beware of the ego and of the complacent attitude. 'I have done it before, and it was alright then.'

Do it once and you are forgiven but be assured that repeated indifference will be seen as defiance.

But your God is a merciful God. He takes no prisoners. All are welcomed into his domain. You are worthy. You are as important as any king in his own kingdom.

So, bide a while on that thought form. If God, in

all his mighty power and busyness is running this vast world, can you not find time to bless and think of him?

46

As she sat by the river on this the sunniest of days, her thoughts floated away on a sea of misty dreams. She had come here for some peace and quiet, for as of recently, her days had been hectic and busy with the family. Her boss had been overdemanding yet again.

'Oh, to escape.' That thought had kept her sane, and so here she was, alone at last, just where she longed to be.

The day drifted on. The sun began to set in the sky. A cool breeze began to blow across the water. 'Time to go,' she thought, 'but not yet'.

She was loath to move. To have to return to her other world seemed daunting, back to all those demands that were made on her time. And yet, would she change it?

Would she have it any other way? To be of use, to be needed, is indeed a blessing, for what is there in life that is more fulfilling than this?

We say, 'No man is an island', but what do we mean by that? Is it of our choosing? Is it from our deep sense of duty that we care for one another?

And yet to be on a desert island can seem like bliss, but of course, there is a downside to all of this. Do we really know what we want or even need?

So, stop a while, and think on that thought.

It is ok to be selfish. You have a need to be selfish. For what you are is human. You are indeed no robot of anyone's making.

So go and dream by your stream or favourite place whenever you can. Escape the rigours of life. Rest awhile and live in that land of bliss. Then come back refreshed, ready and willing to give of yourself. Peace is yours.

That inner strength that others admire in you is so easy to gain if only we remember to stop and 'smell the roses' or 'sail our boats to distant shores'.

47

I know that many of you sit and wait. You wait for God to move in his mysterious ways. You sit and wait for a miracle to make you well, to make you rich or to find a way out of a sticky situation.

And what happens while you sit and wait? Your tempers flare, and your moods become one of despair. You believe that he has forgotten you. We, in our child-like minds, in our blinkered way, can only see as far as the end of our noses.

Go beyond all reason, go beyond the dreams of possibilities, see far into the future, and dare to risk the impossible.

Can you not see? Will you not see that choices are there for your taking? Believe in yourself. Do not rely on the probabilities, the ratio, or the turn of a wheel. Grab onto the belief that you can take charge, that the power is within you.

For you are much more than surface, much more than skin and bone. The power that lies deep within your soul can move mountains. You only have to believe. You only have to have faith, and it will be so.

Grow tall in this belief and see and judge for yourself. You can work with the Master. You are as powerful as the Master.

I see the lack that is all around me. I see the apathy and despair that you think you are in. So, Dear Hearts, dig deep within your psyche, feel deep into the core of your soul, and see that place that is in darkness now, but once the door has been opened to the light, see how the shadows of despair vanish.

Keep that door open. Do not let the light escape.

Once the lock has been turned and the door springs open, you will never want to return to the shadows again.

48

Dear Hearts, let us begin to see the beauty that is all around us. To open our eyes to what is really there, the things that matter to the soul.

Not the amount of litter that blows about your streets. Not the amount of dog foul or chewing gum that makes polka dots on your walkways. See for the first time that tree you have passed many times on your way into town. See its shape and know what type of tree it is. Does it shed its leaves, and do flowers ever appear on its branches?

What of the many gardens that you pass on your travels? Do you even notice the flowers? Even if the garden contains flowers are they in bloom? Do birds ever appear to your listening sense? Is the blare of traffic more in your focus?

Go beyond the obvious. Look, really look at what the opposite has to offer you. You in the mundane everyday world miss so much. You miss that God is trying to give you balance, balance in all things.

Take the good with the bad. That is life. That is the law – equality in all things.

But is it how we see and judge our world? It is not dwelling too much on one without it overshadowing the other: yin and yang.

I go back to my first statement. A gentle reminder, is your glass half full or half empty?

Your answer depends on how your soul and heart see life. Is it a glorious mystery? Or is it a never-ending drudge that once over, then and only then can peace be found?

So please, may I ask this of you? Next time in your life when the sun refuses to shine and when all is blackness, look for one thing, one small spark that lets in the light. Then sit back and watch what happens.

49

It began like any other normal day. Washing pots. More washing. Cooking and cleaning until the house shone like a new pin.

'There,' she thought. 'All is ready. All is done. The rest of the day is mine.'

But what was she to do with this day? Friends had disappeared from the scene long ago. The bully of a husband had seen to that.

'Never mind,' she thought. 'I shall go for a walk.'

Tripping down the lane, she felt at peace with herself and her little world. Gone were the days of stress and despair, of not daring to go out in case people saw the bruises. But that is all in the past. All forgotten, never to go down there again.

The road wound down the bank, down to the stream. The water was running high, as much rain had fallen of late. She slowed her walking down to a gentle saunter. This felt good. This felt real. She breathed out a sigh. 'Yes'. All was at peace in her life.

She found an old shoe, one that had seen better days. 'Like me,' she thought and smiled at the irony of it.

She was about to throw it away when something caught her eye. Something looked very familiar about this shoe. It reminded her of a pair of shoes that she had owned. Could it be? No, that's impossible. So many people must have worn this style, this size and colour. And yet? And yet, the coincidence bemused her.

Was this a message? Was this a sign, a lesson she was meant to understand?

She stood awhile and contemplated the shoe. Why had it returned to her? Why now? What was to understand? What was the message?

Her desire was to throw away the shoe, but she couldn't. Here was puzzlement. Did the shoe represent her? Old, downtrodden, faded and worn out? But that was the old her. That was how she had felt before.

'Yes, that was the old me.' This tattered object that she now held in her hands did represent her.

'But no more.' She smiled.

How she did shout out in triumph when she let go of the shoe, flinging it as far away from herself as she could. With it went all the past hate that the shoe had represented.

She looked down at her feet. 'Yes,' she thought. 'I am wearing my *new shoes*.'

50

As you know, today is special. Why is it so special? It's because you are in it. Yes, YOU! You are as special as is this day. Do you not believe me? Why not? Do you think you are not worthy of this day? Do you think that being so small a creature, you have little or no importance in the scheme of things?

NEVER.

Is not the ant in his colony of other ants just as important, each doing a different job, each one of equal importance?

Think on this, then. Consider this. Why are you here? Why were you born? To answer your calling? The dependency others have on you? Yes, I see a glimmer of realisation. Yes, you begin to understand.

There are times, though, when your life seems mundane, and it all becomes too heavy for you to bear. Perhaps the world does not need you. That the world would be better off without you?

Caring for others is such a burden, too big a responsibility. But stop for one moment and consider, where would the world be without you?

Something you had never considered before? Does it make you smile that one, just one person depends on you for friendship, for guidance, for expertise that you possess in running a household?

All are important. All are as necessary as ruling a kingdom and being Prime Minister.

Their glory may be obvious, but your glory is just as valuable and just as necessary as theirs.

Each of us, in our own way, depends on the other. For what is good and just for one, the other sees fit to be the other.

So never decry your position in life. For though being a small cog in a large wheel, the clock would not work if you were missing.

51

'Eat your tea slowly,' said Mother. 'Do you know that eating in a rush causes wind, most unpleasant?'

The poor child had been waiting so long for its food that speed and gratitude were all that concerned him. The food placed before him was adequate, just the right balance in amount and nutrition.

The poor child had been found wandering, cold and lost in the street, abandoned by his mother and family. But this dear old soul had rescued him and seen his needs. The least she could do, for she had no children of her own and had never been blessed with a family. Her longings had been kept hidden.

As she looked at the child, small she suspected for its age, with large eyes trying so hard to please, her heart leapt out with longing to hold and love this child as any other mother would. But she held back. That wouldn't do. Not good to be seen as sentimental. Her upbringing had seen to that. And yet? And yet to deny what she was feeling, was that so wrong?

Clearing her throat, she asked if the child was finished, had it had enough? She was greeted by a half smile and a gentle nod.

What to do now? Let the child go and seek its parents? The child seemed too afraid of her to speak.

She held out her hand to the child. It quickly slipped from the chair, ran over to her and slipped a hand into hers. It felt warm, and it shook a little. The poor thing was frightened.

What was to happen to him now? He felt a surge of love and gratitude for this fine lady, but not as much as if it was his own mother.

They looked at each other, eyeing each other up and down, both wondering what to do next and neither of them wanting to part.

The situation was resolved by a ringing at the door. The maid answered and in rushed a young girl very distressed, very dishevelled.

'Matthew, Matthew, you are here. We thought we had lost you,' she cried.

The boy rushed from the old lady into the arms of his real mother. With a smile and a backward glance, they were gone.

The old lady watched them depart. There was no need for thanks or gratitude, for it seemed so natural.

The reason why we are here, the need for 'mothers' of the world to simply be here for whosever child is in need or distress.

This is why the Earth is so lovingly named 'Mother Earth', for does she not supply each one of us, whoever, wherever we dwell on this planet, without asking for any thanks?

52

'As you know,' said Mary, 'all is not well at home'.

'Sorry to hear of that,' said Jane. 'Can I be of any help?'

'My dear friend, you are indeed the kindest of souls, but no. This is something that the family must sort out. They will have to learn that I cannot be all things to everybody.'

'So be it, my friend, but remember I am here whenever you have a need of me.' At this, the friends parted.

Much later, they happened to meet again, and the conversation again got around to family matters.

'Have things improved in your household, Mary?' Jane asked.

'Yes indeed, peace and tranquillity now reign.'

'Well done, indeed I am pleased.'

Seeing her friend so upset yet unable to help was a great worry for Jane. But all is resolved. All is at peace.

Do you know of a friend or an acquaintance who is troubled by such things?

'How can I help?' you may ask when help is not needed, just by being there when a need arises. Wait and see can be the hardest when a loved one is troubled. But it is in the waiting that love and healing takes place.

See others as they see you. Watch and listen for keywords, then act upon them.

To be a great listener is perhaps all that is needed. For when this happens, do we not see for ourselves the healing that is taking place?

So go. Be the best you can be. Have patience. Sit and wait. Just being there is the most that you can be.

Do not see it as a burden. See it as a compliment that you are indeed the most trusted of souls. Maybe someday you too will need a listening friend, and where would you turn to?

53

As you sit and contemplate your life from where you started to where you are now, are you pleased that life has given you many opportunities to shine? What things about your life make you proud?

Consider your place in this world. Consider your friends and family. Could you have played your part any differently?

Is it just by chance that fortune has smiled on you? Is it by chance that the 'great spirit' who watches over you, your benevolent 'Father', has seen fit to bestow his grace on you? Or are you at a loss with your life? Are you angry at being denied what you thought was rightfully yours? Envious of your neighbour, why him and not me?

Go inside. Go deep down into that place and see the spark of life. That deep well. A place you may have never dared to venture. But try. Please try.

What do you see? Is there something lacking there? Is it an empty spot, or is it a full and warm place?

Confused by all of this?

To understand what I am trying to explain, what I am trying to make you understand is that perhaps the judgement you have of others is so misplaced that you do not see the wood for the trees.

I don't wish to confuse you. I don't wish to blame you, but the illogic of your thought pattern is causing you much grief and anguish.

Relax. Do not see others as 'having it all'. Their needs are not yours. Their world may be on the outside, all 'grace and favour', but do you not see or understand that maybe their world is not as 'special' as others see it?

'You would like to try their world', I hear you say.

'To live in luxury just once, to give it a try, perhaps.' But perhaps not. For your place in the world is, as ever, just as important. Your place is just where you are at this very moment.

Do not waste your time on foolish dreams. Live your life as it has been given to you.

For dreams are all well and good. Some dreams do come true. Some do not.

Are we the worse for it if sudden wealth evades us? Are we any the less deprived by having not gained that long-awaited goal?

Time is on your side. Time to be who you were meant to be, chosen only when the time is 'right'. When you are ready and capable of attaining your reward.

Until then, live and grow. For it is in the learning along the way that, once the goal is achieved, we can hold onto that moment. And know that we, and we alone, have 'grown' in God's favour.

Blessed is he who acknowledges the divine in all things achieved.

God blessed and smiled on all souls who sought knowledge. Seek to achieve the goals in life, be it love, family or work.

So be contented with your lot. For riches of the soul are more valuable than all the wealth in the land.

54

'Dearly beloved, we are gathered here in the presence of God to join these two people in Holy Matrimony' and so forth.

The joining of two people together, how well does that sit with you?

Two people who love come together to be as one. One with each and one with God.

Does this thought seem to be a bit outdated, outmoded in this 21st century? Are the old ways outdated? Does ritual of past times seem archaic to you?

Vows that are readily taken can be so easily broken. It seems that marriage is just a formality that society expects for the sake of propriety and future children.

According to the marriage ceremony, it must be entered soberly and with honesty, forsaking all others. Can you see, or not as the case may be, that a commitment of such magnitude is not for the faint-hearted? I see amongst many of you that the piece of paper that is given to you at the end as proof of such a commitment is simply 'not worth the effort. Why go through all that stress just to make it legal when that proof of our commitment is there for all to see?'

As we travel through our lives, when life becomes too much and when loyalty to one another is no more, what do we have? We have no foundation of belief or commitment. Where is the rock that we can depend on?

Is that piece of paper just what it seems to be, merely an old scrap of innate words? Or is it your rock, your foundation of the commitment you have made?

Many people will judge you either way, with or without your public commitment, but your soul knows. It honours the commitment you have made.

Do not run away at the first whiff of deceit, rage, or discontentment. See and grow. You have planted the seed now. Watch it grow and blossom into something fine.

See your seedling grow into a fine upstanding tree with many blossoms. There will be times when leaves are shed, but this is all in the growing. This is how life was meant to be. When tears fall, when the season of autumn sets in, it's time to take stock of where you are together in this life.

There are many seasons in our lives. Autumn is but one of them. Grow from that time, for soon it will be spring. Soon it will be your summer. And winter?

Well, winter is for old age when love is mellow. When there is need for little growth. For the tree of your life has reached its maturity.

55

'Shall we begin today with a prayer?' said the vicar to his small congregation.

'We are here today to bless each and every one of us gathered here to be together on this wonderful sunny day in spring. Dear Lord, grant us thy blessings. Grant us the wisdom of thy knowledge so we can live our lives in thee. Amen.'

The service continued until all the hymns were sung and the processional had retired into the transept.

A cheery 'Good morning' was the last thing the vicar said to Mary as she went home.

Home was not the same now that Fred had gone. Home to her was just a shelter from the weather – a haven to lay her head down.

Friends were fine, loyal and true, but they could not compensate for the companionship of her Fred.

'But life goes on,' she had told herself. And it had. For much that she had thought had been taken away from her now was returning.

No more the quiet, obedient wife. She now enjoyed a sense of freedom, of release from the pattern of being the 'dutiful wife'.

Little by little, she sensed the change in her. She seemed to laugh more. She was coming out of the shadows.

Fred had been a good provider. A strong dominant character, which made her feel good, safe and secure. She asked nothing in life but to be the one who looked after her 'Fred'.

But now that he was gone, what role was she to play?

Freedom can be a little scary when one has not known it for so long. Freedom to be who you truly are, to speak what is in your heart and mind without the approval of others.

Intimidation is the cruellest form of oppression. We see this in so many disguises.

Go back to being a child, when the first thoughts that popped into our heads were spoken – no need for the approval of anybody.

As we grow and characters are formed, the influences of others take priority. Then, when we let others dominate for the sake of 'peace and quiet', we do ourselves much harm.

The solution? Are you brave enough to reach the solution? To go beyond what is expected of you? To step out of the shadows once more to voice, to let that little voice be heard?

Be as a child. I dare you to do it. I dare you to be what your heart longs you to be.

Are you prepared 'to do or die?' Perhaps one day?

56

As Jesus once said, 'Ye reap what you sow.'

How well does it sit with you? Are you a believer or a non-believer? Is it a truth that is as old as the hills or a benign jest of some ancient sage?

Think back to a time, a time when revenge was all that filled your mind. 'To do unto others as they see fit to do to you.'

Was it easy? Was it a just and noble cause that you were on, a warrior, righting the wrongs of the foe?

Is revenge a worthy cause? Is it a satisfying substitute for reasoning?

Think about this the next time you seek your revenge. Wait until the 'dust settles', then consider the alternative.

Do not be hasty in your judgement. Try to see what was behind the other's intent. Try to be in their shoes. What made them react that way? Indeed, you will be surprised at the 'alternative'.

In your haste, in your quickness to blame, to react with revenge, we miss an opportunity for understanding.

Do you want someone's 'death' on your conscience? I speak bluntly to you, be it one or any army of revengeful people.

Please consider this. Be as a small child. Not in a cowardly mode. Not in a feeble vain, but in a slow, logical mind. A mind of reasoning that, having once made your move, there is no going back.

Once the confrontation has begun, there is no going back. Pride is now the issue. Pride, in all its glory, will rear its ugly head. A 'do or die' situation takes place. Retreat is not an option.

Haste is not for the brave. Haste and revenge are the fool's way. The wise man considers all his options and then acts upon them.

'He who hesitates is lost', I hear you say.

Perhaps. Perhaps not. But consider this the next time when confronted with revenge. He who seeks the stone, the first stone that is thrown, will he be prepared to repay the damage?

57

It is said, 'He that is without blame, let him throw the first stone.'

Is that a just and fair statement? Does your conscience seek to understand it? Does your ego see the logic that is behind the statement?

Many of you may wish to debate this. Many of you will seek not even to judge whether it is a fair statement or not.

Go deeper into this parable and see. Try your understanding in all its many different facets.

Are you only looking with the eyes of a child or the eyes of one who sees many parallels to this conundrum?

It is always so easy to judge another. To throw scorn on any situation with or without knowing all the facts. In your haste to judge, we forget the one thing we should not. We should not like to see ourselves in this same situation.

It is so easy to sit in judgement of others from afar, not easily involved. It is only when we are close up to the perpetrators does our logic and curiosity seek out knowledge of the 'other side'.

To be judge and jury before knowing the facts is, in itself, farcical.

What right have we, of lesser worth, ever to think that our opinions of the self are any less than those of the arbitrator?

Judge not those amongst you that fail society. What are we but children of any lesser God than those who seek to abuse you?

The Father sees all. He alone knows of the failings of others. Theirs is a lesson that must be learned in a time-honoured way.

Be as Solomon. Be as wise as him. Judge not

others for, even though they know what they do. We, who condemn them, are as one with a closed mind.

The perpetrators who seek out to cause revenge only do so because theirs is the guilty conscience.

Next time we seek revenge, when we seek anarchy, stop and consider this. Who, indeed, is ready to pick the first stone?

Who amongst you knows all the facts, knows that he has not been there before in that same situation?

58

To increase one's knowledge is indeed a longing of the soul.

Do not deny your appetite that the soul craves.

Knowledge is not power in the broadest sense. It leads to an understanding of fellow man. It opens up even more questions that need to be answered.

To seek knowledge is indeed a blessing.

A seeker of knowledge is likened to a small child that needs to grow and develop until he can teach others.

When all the knowledge of the Earth is gathered together, man, in his wisdom, will be in touch with his very soul. Then he can live amongst the stars.

Go and seek all the masters. Learn from them, but then reach that bit further on into your own psyche, for there is your truth and nothing but your truth.

59

It is said, 'All who are heavy laden, who come to me, I will give them rest.'

Who are these seekers of 'rest?' who amongst you are willing to trust and bear with me in their quest for help?

Does not the 'will' of those that battle against all odds, those that are feeling lost and forsaken, seem so set in their ways that the thought of outside help simply does not exist? They struggle and fret, losing many a sleepless night in the quest for answers.

My dear children, I am here. I am waiting to give you rest. Resist the struggles. Cease the conflict that your heart longs to find. I am waiting. Waiting to shoulder that burden. You were never meant to walk alone.

Why try to be brave and soldier on? Why struggle against the tide that seeks to wash you away?

I watch, I see, and I long to be of help. How often must you sink below the surface before asking for help?

Do you think that no one is there, no one is listening, and no one can hear you?

I watch and wait. I long to be needed by you.

I have a duty of care for all my children. Would not any loving parent give all for his children?

Believe. You only have to simply believe that you are being cared for. Reach out to me, for I am only a thought away.

Do not struggle so. You are never alone in any crisis. You were never meant to be alone.

For it is not written that all who call on me, call my name, I am with them?

So, Dear Heart, remember. Remember me next time, this time, anytime in your trials of life, for I am here. I am waiting for your call.

60

A star is born today. A bright shining star.

'Who is this star?' you may ask, 'and where is it that this so-called 'star' is being born?'

Imagine, just imagine. Let your thought flow in the air. Go and dream on a wave of sweet bliss. Go to an imaginary plane where all is peaceful, all is harmonious, and all is perfect. It is not so hard to do. We all love to daydream, to let our imagination drift on a sea of tranquillity. So off we go into the distant horizon.

Are you there yet? Have you reached the shore? Have you landed in your new world?

Look around you. What do you see? What do you feel? Is this where you would like to be, where you would like to stay? Living at this level is bliss. Being in this state of suspension, is it but a dream?

Dwell for a while. Come back rejuvenated. Come back? Why not remain on this wavelength? Does life have to be any different from this? Does the bubble have to burst?

Reality for you may seem mundane. We only have to look outside ourselves to see true reality. To connect both worlds, that is the key, that is true reality.

So what about your star? The star that has just been born? YOU are that 'star'. You are a star in the making. Do you not see that to live between these two worlds is where you were meant to be?

You are puzzled, I see, but think on this. Your DNA, your molecular structure, is the same as the stars. The compound is the same, so why be surprised? Why shake your head in disbelief?

It is YOU that is the 'star', the STAR that is born today.

61

Do you like where you live, the place you call home? Does it fill your needs? Is it your shelter from the storm, or just somewhere you happen to hang your hat?

What of the people that share your home? Are they happy to be there? Does harmony fill your days, or are there constant quarrels and slamming of doors?

What of your neighbours? Do they greet you with a cheery 'hello' and are willing to babysit for you when needed?

What of your street, your town? Does it vibrate with an energy that says 'welcome' to all strangers?

Be honest now. Let's not pretend.

Perhaps the street is not as clean as it could be. Perhaps the roads have potholes. Do abandoned cars litter the waste ground? Look and see. Look again at your town. What improvements could be made?

Perhaps you would like to see flowers everywhere, hanging baskets from lampposts, and less graffiti?

Go back to your street. Go back inside your house. Go deep inside to your very soul. Do you like what you see?

What changes would you like to see happen? Can you even bear to change? Do you even want to?

What is so good about you? Be honest now. Let's not pretend.

If you do not like what you see, it can be changed. It can vibrate to a different tune.

You can sow the seeds of change. For when you do, see how the flowers will grow.

62

How has your day been, this bright and glorious day you have been given?

Have you sailed on a tidal wave, bobbing along merrily, achieving all you desired?

Have all the people that you have met greeted you with a smile and a wave?

As you come to the end of this day, do peace and quiet invade your soul?

Does the quietness of this twilight time make you reflect on all the achievements of this day? Are you pleased with your life? Does gratitude to Him who watches over you sit on your lips?

Be at peace now. Let that feeling flow over you. Let it wash over you, filling you with a sense of gratitude that this place at this very moment is where you were meant to be.

You are my beloved child. You are that flower that grows well in my garden. Know that you are well cared for and that I never neglect my garden. For each one of you is my chosen bloom, my prized possession.

63

Are you well this day? Are you happy and healthy on this glorious day? Does all around you seem at ease? Do you take for granted this beautiful morning?

Is your life, your attitude this 'of course I am alive. I expect no other?'

To be taken for granted may not seem a bad thing, just to know that your tomorrows will always dawn.

As we continue down the road in this life, we rarely contemplate our journey's end. I do not wish to be gloomy on such a beautiful day, but just stop for a moment and consider that perhaps tomorrow for you will never dawn. How would you spend your last day if you knew that your tomorrows had ceased?

Panic? Hurriedly say you're sorry? Right all the wrongs that have been troubling you?

DO IT NOW. Do it now, for time is not on your side. Make that peace with whoever troubles you.

See that perhaps, just this once, you make the first move. Do not delay, for this day may be your last.

For your life is but a gift, freely given with great love, but a present that should not be taken for granted.

64

How many times a day do you look down at your feet?

Consider your feet for a moment. Are they too large, too small, too broad, bony and pointed, bits sticking out here and there? Do you ever thank your feet for the hard work that they do? Or do you take them for granted, getting you from A to B?

Feet are very important. I am sure you will agree. How do we stand up to be counted if we have no feet to do so?

Have you ever considered what it must be like to be born without two feet? With one, you could at least hop about, but no feet! Do you see my problem?

Was there a time when you, let's say, damaged one of your feet? How did you survive? Was it easy? Did you have someone to go and fetch for you? Consider living on your own. How, then, would you have managed?

Go back in time to when, as a baby, you were learning to walk. Remember all the bumps and bruises? But once mastered, oh, the freedom to be able to run and jump with such balance. You felt as if you were the master of your own body.

What I am trying to say is that perhaps we forget our achievements. We forget all the trials we have won, and we only see what the next one is to be.

So, take not the trials in our lives as a baby would, with tears and tantrums, bumps and bruising. Learn and be grateful that, perhaps, it is just that we take life for granted.

For learning to stand on our own two feet, is that not the lesson we were sent here for?

65

What I want to say today is simply this. Are you who you think you are?

Are you so pleased with yourself that your life is of your own making? Does all seem to you at this time all smiles and roses?

Consider this. Consider choice. Consider the whereabouts you were born. Would you have played the game of life any other way? Has fate dealt you a good hand? Many questions and many answers. But this can depend on, let's say, how you are feeling today. How rich you are. Whether you are sick or in good health. Whether the sun is shining or not. Influences of other people, siblings or family, friends or the boss.

Look in the mirror. What do you see? Who do you see? Who is really looking back at you?

Does it please you the image that is reflected there? Look deeper into the eyes. Perhaps you smile. Perhaps you frown.

Do you see a 'friend?' Are you angry at the flaws that seem to plague you, wishing for perfection?

Resist the temptation of criticism. What you see is just a vessel, just a carcass for you to live in.

It is not the real you. The real you lives deep below the surface. What you and everybody else sees and recognises is just the form that you have developed over the years so that others may recognise the outer casing.

It is of no great consequence, its shape or colour, male or female, large or small, infirmed with a handicap. The body will pass away. It will decay and die. It will return to dust, but your soul will live on. So, judge not another by their appearance.

For there is a saying, 'judge not a book by its cover', for once that book has been opened, oh, what surprises await us. What discoveries are to be made once its pages are read?

65A

I looked into the mirror
That's not me.
The tired old woman with white hair
That's not me.
That woman who can hardly see
That's not me.

I am a fairy that dances at the bottom of a garden,
I fly over the trees on an exciting journey.
I am bursting with sheer delight because my soul is
free.
That's me.

66

I have a story I wish to relate to you. A story, which you may or not believe in, it all depends on where and what your aims for a better world are.

There once was a lonely and sickly boy, the youngest of a large family. Though he was much loved by his parents, his siblings took great delight in treating him with contempt and derision.

He bore his place in society with great dignity, never defending himself or retaliating.

As he grew and became a man, his chances of succeeding in becoming what his heart desired seemed to him to be a distant dream and only a dream.

His older brothers saw less and less of him, never including him in their social activities. His sisters treated him like a baby or as the unpaid servant of the house.

Time passed. He hid his secret longings until one day, just by chance, he saw the advert in the local newspaper.

'Wanted. Strong farm labourer. Must be used to hard outdoor work. Small wage but includes board and lodgings.'

'This is just what I have been waiting for,' he thought. He applied and got his wish.

But to tell his parents! The agony of telling his brothers and sisters was the worst part. He took courage in both hands, stood his ground, and blurted out what he had done.

Oh, how they laughed. Oh, how they called him a fool. Their cruelty knew no bounds.

The day came for him to leave. Little was said, for his expectance of returning home they thought was imminent. Off he went, never to be seen again.

The family looked for him, searching every outlet they could think of. He could not be traced.

Years passed. It was as if he had never existed. (Was there ever a Simon? Was there ever a young son that waited on the household?)

Regrets were many now. Regrets of lost opportunity, never to have known their younger brother.

Does any of my story ring true to you? You with your busy days, busy ways of living your life?

Is there someone you have forgotten about, treated less kindly than you should have?

Sometimes we all get bogged down with the busyness of our small world that we forget that someone is just waiting to hear from us, to recognise his or her existence.

Who waits for your call? Who longs to be by your side? It's not too late, is it?

67

'Hello, Dad,' shouted the girl.

The old man lifted his head to recognise that familiar voice. 'Hi, Stacy. Glad you are here. I am having a bit of bother.'

'Now, what have you been up to? Can't do without me, eh?' replied the girl.

'None of your cheek now,' came the reply.

Stacy, his beloved daughter, the apple of his eye, was all that was left now of his family. They were all gone. Some had died. The rest had moved away to find work. But Stacy had stayed, not out of kindness, but out of a loving heart for the old man. Her life was on hold until she was needed elsewhere.

The banter continued, each relying on the other for companionship. The truth is that one needed the other.

Nothing much exciting happened in their lives. The need for excitement was unnecessary, for they had each other for as long as necessary.

Days plodded on, and the routine never changed until one day, as if an omen had been predicted, Stacy didn't appear at the door. Confused by this, the old man, not given to worrying, became alarmed. Panic set in.

'Where was she? She's never been late before. Must have slept in. Not like her.' The hours crept by. 'What to do, who do I tell? I need help. I haven't had my breakfast yet.'

All was confusion for the old man.

He realised all too late his dependency on his daughter. She was his lifeline to the outside world. How was he to cope, shop, cook and clean?

Terror consumed him. He wanted to leave with

his beloved daughter (for, other than death, was the reason she was not here).

Sitting in the gloom, never having moved from his chair, he fell into a deep sleep and began dreaming.

He dreamed of his beloved Stacy when she was a small child. She used to climb upon his knee. His 'special girl' he had called her.

Then she was old. Old as he was now. Very strange. It must be a lack of food.

Then Stacy did appear to him, calling him by his first name.

'Harold, hi! Harold, it's all right. Nothing to fear. I am waiting for you. Take my hand. I have been waiting. Death is not so bad. All is beautiful here. No more aches and pains, together at last.'

He smiled. 'Oh,' he thought, 'am I dead? No one told me. And our Stacy. Does she know?'

'Yes, my dear. We all know.'

68

How are you this day? Is all well in your life? Does wisdom and knowledge for others flow gently from your lips?

Do you see and understand that the wisdom you relate is not necessary from you, that you are indeed guided by a higher spiritual being?

Now, come down to earth. Now see for yourself that only the pure in heart are the 'earth masters'. That is who we guide and tender. Not necessarily the 'chosen ones' but the seekers of wisdom. The need to know the truth of 'what is?'

One question leads to another, and so on.

That life is eternal. Not one of you on your Earth plane knows of the joys that await you once you have stepped outside from the heavy energies you now dwell in.

Put aside all thoughts of disquiet and all thoughts of 'what ifs'. See for yourself the richness, the bounteousness of the gifts that lie dormant deep within your psyche.

Do not seek to be a leader of men. Do not stand out from the crowd or draw attention. Be as the rarest orchid. Once found, its beauty can be admired.

As I see it, the workings of man, the strife that is caused all in the name of justice and fairness, to bang one's 'drum', to be who shouts the loudest, does not necessarily get the job or the problem solved.

I do not wish to deter those of you who see no other way to achieve your goal, the desired results at all costs, but for those who dwell in the 'light', a softer, gentler approach is equally as effective.

Be the 'gentle warrior'. Go silently through your day, gently wafting your essence as you go amongst others.

Force versus force only leads to conflict. Gentle persuasion, a gentle breath on the lips. See if that works.

For who knows the art of gentle persuasion better than your Father?

69

We shall begin today with a story. A story that is as 'old as the hills', you may say. Some may believe, but others chose not to take on board the advice I now reiterate. So, let's begin.

It was a day just as today, when all was at peace, the sun shining and the sky blue. All was well with her world. Lost in her daydreaming of future events, plans that had been made long ago, of a holiday to far distant shores.

Then the phone rang. Disaster. A much-loved one had died suddenly. Gone was the dream. Her bubble had burst.

Hurried plans were made, and duty had been done. She returned to her planned life.

Contemplating this in her dreamtime, she reflected on her mortality. How little time, how little knowledge she had of such an eventuality of her own death, a fear that she was not prepared for her own departure from this Earth. She needed to set her life in order, to know that preparations for such an event were in order.

'Strange,' she thought, 'that now, at this very moment, it seemed logical to set to rights all that she could for such an event.'

The mood passed. The thought was just a distant memory until, once more, death invaded her life. Not her own, but yet again, it dislodged the old pattern of not being prepared.

Is death an issue with you, my dear reader? Does it flit across your consciousness and then leave just as quickly?

Is it just fear? Is it such a taboo subject that it's

only the old and depressed that need to listen?

Look at this day. See its beauty. See the birds and animals. See nature at its best. Is that all there is? Could there be more?

My dears, what joys await you. What bliss is yet to come, the like of which you cannot imagine. Be not afraid. Be assured that life in its progression (for that is what death is) is within your reach.

Today may not be a good day or the time for you to contemplate this subject. Maybe in your reverie, it will come to pass, a fleeting glimpse, a thought form that will pass lightly across your mind. Hold onto it for just a moment longer. Hold it just there and be not afraid, for there is much love, such a sense of freedom that just maybe you have nothing to fear.

So, take my hand, and I will lead you to a place where all is warm and happy, where tears are no more, where only love and joy await you, and where I wait for you.

Smile and be not afraid.

70

The day came, the day that she had been dreading. Fighting this feeling of dread that welled up inside of her was all that she could do to stop herself from being sick.

The thought that they were going to take away her baby, that they could even contemplate such a horrific act, made her blood run cold.

This is not a pretty picture I paint. This is not the nightmare that dreams are made of. This is reality in all its ugliness.

What had she done to warrant such a situation? What dreadful deed had made the law, in its infinite wisdom, seek to judge this state of events?

Poverty, my dear friend. Poverty. The curse of the weak and the dispossessed.

Judge not those that dwell among you, for in doing so, you are as guilty as those that prey on the weak and the vulnerable.

What can one do in such a situation?

Empty your pockets? Seek revenge on the authorities? Or open your hearts? For the gift of love costs you nothing, but it is everything.

71

As you sit and contemplate this day away from your busy outside world, does the reason why you were born ever cross your mind? The wonder of it all, that you, at this very moment, exist?

Was it chance that, just because two souls saw fit to join together, you are the result?

We could argue that just because 'nature called' and I am a result of it, that is all there is to it. Simple! And yet, no. Life is simple. The making of a new life is not of your making, but of the God force or nature herself, for she is of no lesser deity than the Creator himself. And there we lead onto another simile.

Are Mother Nature and God the same being? Do we see them as separate or consider that they are 'one'?

In the animal kingdom, they have their 'season'. Is it just by chance that they know it's spring? Or is it the God force within them that sees new offspring being born?

Man, in his wisdom, has no 'season', so it is just by random choice that new babies are born. Just a hit-and-miss affair? Precautions are necessary when choices have to be made. This we understand.

But consider this. Does 'love' drive the animal kingdom? Does companionship exist and have meaning?

We, who see man as a higher being, a creature of great intellect who plays around with 'nature', sometimes never considering their actions or the result of them, as creatures of great folly.

But all is not lost. Choices are being made. We

look to see that what they experience, other than pleasure, is the responsibility that they follow through with. The need a soul has at such times is to bring into force the concept that he and only he is the creator of the next generation.

Be of good cheer about such things. The Lord, your God, looks down with a benevolent smile, for he knows that man, in his wisdom, is but a lesser seeker of knowledge. He longs to believe that he and he alone has the power of creation. Nature, though, in her wisdom, rules wisely, for she knows her limitations.

72

It came to pass that this day was no ordinary day, for it seemed to her a day when all her belief system had been put to the test.

Gone were the 'ifs and buts' to be replaced by the stronger beliefs of a knowledge she had not thought possible.

Doubts began to creep into her mind. Was this for real? Had she 'flipped her lid' as others had suspected? To go against the flow, to seek the alternative route, does that take bravery? Does that seem like 'death by your own destruction?'

Lonely though the road may seem, for others may long to join you but do not know how, it is a road that runs through all eternity through many lives.

The road is a lonely one, and yet you are never alone. The God force that is your very breath sees that many masters are there at your calling.

So be not afraid. Fear is the dark side of joy.

Be not overwhelmed by the synchronicity of life.

When 'dark' times appear and progress is slow, accept, reflect, and let not your eagerness build to frustration. It is not a battle. It is not a race. To learn the lesson well, then and only then can progress succeed.

Never see your 'dark' times as a punishment. They are but your times of rest and revolution.

As you progress, when you reach the next plane of your existence, what joy will that bring? You see a different view. A different world is yours. So live in that 'world' for a while. Enjoy its warmth and

expectations, but remember with joy in your heart
how you got there.

May your sense of achievement be your reward.
Be not contented to dwell too long, for how many
other worlds are waiting for you to explore.

73

There once was a little boy, a beautiful baby loved by all. He grew up to be a teacher. He was loved by all his pupils and by all who knew him.

His calling was to serve all. A conviction that he was born out of dedication to be of service.

His life progressed in order and correction. Little were his joys along the way, until one day, just by chance, he found himself sitting on a park bench next to a tramp, a 'gentleman of the road'.

Eyeing each other up and down, not knowing what to say, they both, in unison, said, 'Good morning, nice day.'

Taken aback, they both retreated into their shells.

Silence.

'Nice weather for this time of the year' was the echo in unison between them.

More silence.

'This cannot go on', they thought – in unison.

'Been here long?' came the joint reply.

Irritation began to bubble through one of them. A chuckle was fermenting in the stomach of the other.

Can you guess which of the two gentlemen was feeling annoyed and which was feeling silly? And why?

Which of the two gentlemen would you like to be?

74

Hold out your hand. What do you see?

'Why my hand, of course', you reply. Is it just a hand, or is it just that extra bit attached to the end of your arm?

Look at your hand. Examine it hard. Look closely. See the wonder of it.

Let your imagination take flight. See it as a wing, a claw with long and short talons.

The use of your hand is obvious. You need a hand to function, true, and yet, no.

Does a rabbit need a hand to hold his food? Does an eagle need to carry his prey in a hand?

Imagine you had no hands. Shudder at the thought? A feeling of loss and panic? See the utter dependency on taking what we consider normal for granted. For without our hands, do we still function? Do we still breathe? Are we still alive?

The point I am making is simply to see, to say to ourselves that though it is our God-given right to be born with two hands and not two heads, it is just the norm for the abnormal that is taken for granted.

Look and see inside yourself. Look and see just what people think and see as normal or abnormal.

To judge what is abnormal by our own standards is to judge others of lesser abilities.

The reasoning may seem deep and ponderous to comprehend the logic behind my story, but rest awhile and consider it.

Consider just how we judge others and the need to judge others. Look down and see your hand as a wonder of creation and a blessing.

Judge not others who are different from us, for what is normal?

75

Why wait, for tomorrow is another day, and as the time is now, do not delay in the impulses that take you away to another dimension.

Go with your instincts. Do not put off till tomorrow what can be done today.

The Lord your God may see fit not to give you the morrow. Then all would be lost. All good intentions have failed you.

76

As you progress through this lifetime, as you journey on your path of life, do you ever dream of a life long forgotten?

By dreaming, I mean awakening to the possibility that you might have travelled down a similar pathway.

Maybe not on this Earth plane. Maybe you travelled in another dimension, away from the norm.

Does your imagination ever wander through the impossible into the realms of the improbable? Does realisation ever become a possibility?

Perhaps the ridiculous abhors you. Stupidity is not to be tolerated. And yet, what are those possibilities, the odds that just maybe? Hold that thought. Let it suspend there in the air above you. How can you be sure that, just perhaps?

Fantasy may not be your strong point.

But to step beyond the everyday concept of what is 'the norm,' is that a different reality? Is that only for the young in heart, those that long for adventure?

Are not your dream adventures your wild imaginings? Man, in all his wonder, is a creature that, if he so chooses, limits himself only by reason. His logical brain maybe dominates over flights of fantasy, but does reality have to be logical?

Why does proving e equals mc squared have anything to do with the possibility of an inquiring mind that seeks to explore the unknown with the purpose of just perhaps there is an alternative?

Go back in time. Go back to the dinosaurs when

they walked this Earth. How do you know of such things? Were you there? Discoveries have been made, and fossils have been found to verify such things. You have the proof, and you accept its logic. So you need proof. You need understanding before you accept this concept that I speak of.

Where to go to find it?

The knowledge, the intellect, that gut feeling that only you and you alone can be sure of, for to deny our very birthright can only do damage to our psyche.

Perhaps I skim over this concept too lightly. Perhaps I have lost you on the way.

To speak plain is not of my choosing, for if the spark of imagination has been rekindled in you, then I have done my job. For it is an awakening that I choose to ignite within you.

I challenge you. I stir the embers of some forgotten place. Somewhere deep behind a closed door that only waits for you to turn the handle and again open up to the possibilities of a long-forgotten moment in which a lifetime of memories come flooding forth.

Be brave, for who knows, once the door has been opened, once the flow begins, where will you have journeyed?

77

He was small. Small in stature, small in his mind. His way of thinking left a lot to be desired.

How many times do you judge and see others in this way? Is life not a mirror? Looking at others, do we not judge them by our own standards?

Who are you that can take such responsibility for the justifications of others?

We know not the situation that has brought them to that way of thinking. Their concept of reality may seem bizarre, but who are we to judge another?

Lay down all your thoughts of prepossession. See and judge not others, for theirs is their own reality.

It may seem bizarre and alien to you, but logic cannot and is not of your understanding when perceived by another. We are all quick to compare, judge, and even ridicule others when in fact, our concept is limited.

Are you so pure in heart? Are you the result of divine intervention? What is the gift that you give so freely? By any other standard, lack is at the forefront.

Harsh words? Words of warning?

I go before you to smooth the pathway ahead. Do not see a rocky road. Do not see the tide that will sweep you along, losing all control, losing your footing and your stability. The rush of water that takes your footing away only seeks to place you on distant shores where all is calm.

I ask you to let others be. Let them see that they judge their own mistakes. For theirs is the lesson of their own making.

Why seek to stress yourself with others and their problems? Are you such a master at solving riddles? Have you not got your own issues to resolve?

Be blessed with the countenance of the Buddha. See him smile. See and know that the secrets he shares are yours for the taking.

For what does a smile cost? What price for letting go and just 'being' and letting others 'be'?

78

As you sit and ponder this day, are you filled with a longing to know who and what you are? What brought you to this Earth plane and why?

Does the thought of your return ever fill you with dread, a foreboding of gloom and pain?

This may not seem to be the subject to discuss on such a bright and cheerful day, but all is necessary in the scheme of things.

Put aside all thoughts of the mundane just for a moment. Go into the realms of probability, the possibility that perhaps you and you alone already know the answers that lay deep within your psyche.

Trust that belief. Accept what your gut reaction tells you, for many have ignored the call and wasted valuable time and heartache on worrying.

The Lord your God sees and knows. He looks at you with a benevolent smile. He longs to spare you the burden of conflict. Age in its entire spectrum, in all its stages, awakens in each of us the ability to see the next decade, to see that road unfolding before us. It can be scary and filled with wonder and hope, but that same wonder can be filled with good things yet to come.

How is that for you? Scary or wondrous? An adventure waiting to happen, or a long and dreary road with a sense of wishing you could see the end in sight? Shame on you if it is so.

We know the heart gets weary when conflict or ill health fills your days. We know that patience is the hardest lesson you have to learn, but once conquered, once the barriers come down and when light floods your heart and soul, the victory is yours.

But how long is your 'piece of string?' I hear you

cry. As long as it takes. As long as you refuse to travel this road alone.

We are waiting to carry you. Release it, and let it go to a higher authority. You will be glad you did.

79

I come today to speak to you in a language as old as time itself. A belief system that many choose to forget. It may sound simple. Too simple for you who are scholars, for those that dwell on a higher plane of thought. Do not sneer or decry those of lesser intellect or knowledge than you.

Knowledge is not only about passing exams, letters after one's name or quoting some great text from an ancient book. Knowledge is about life. It's about all the experiences one has gone through and the lessons one has learnt on life's journey.

In their infant wisdom, the young may stumble and rebel against authority, but theirs is the learning of life. Theirs is the understanding of justice and tradition.

As we in the so-called 'adult stage', are we any less able to set the example needed?

Knowledge and proof of such wisdom has to be seen from both sides of the equation. Knowledge and justice may, to some, be the same side of the coin, but is it? Is it just a convenient ploy to keep lesser souls in their place?

They say, 'knowledge is power'. Who says this? Is it some egotistic bigwig that seeks to win his argument or some blatantly naïve snob who seeks to blind and dominate his argument?

Do not be deceived by such power. Your truth, your belief system, is as powerful as any. Your experience of life has taught you your own power structure. Stand by that belief. Stand up and be counted, for your soul knows your very truth.

Be not overwhelmed by people who bombard

you with advice, for it is only their opinions, their belief system. Be your own judge. Listen to their philosophy. Judge it on its merit. Then and only then, begin to see if it makes sense to your understanding.

We are all eager to give advice, and rightly so. We all long to ease another's burden. But it is in the manner of our giving with a loving heart and not as a dictatorial father.

If advice is not received well, stand back and leave well alone. Let that, and all thoughts, hang there waiting to be acted upon. If the giver gives with his heart, he has done all that is asked of him.

80

Are you happy this day? Is life, for you, all that you expected?

No? Then ask yourself why. Why does this life not meet all that you had asked for?

Do you reach for that star, that goal, that dream that always seems to be out of your reach?

Is impatience your strongest point? Do you think of 'giving up', for all seems a waste of time and energy?

Do not see yourself as being of any less perfection than those already 'there', those that have already climbed their mountain and are now residing amongst the stars. (How do you know how many lifetimes it has taken them to do so?)

Time is not the issue here. Frustrating as time to you may seem. It is the journey, not the 'resting place', that is all-consuming and all-powerful. That is the reason you are alive. That makes your awareness of being in the 'now'.

What is the hurry? Is it the case of competition of being like your neighbour, admired?

May I ask why you have this compulsion to be as others are? You are unique. You are the very blessed child of God. He does not need clones. He does not demand or seek to compare. For remember, you are made in his image.

For the Lord your God is likened to a diamond, a multi-cut diamond. And you! Yes, YOU are one of his many facets.

Go and shine, for you are his child. You are part of the whole.

81

The child was angry. Very angry. Nothing his mother could do would placate him.

Fighting and screaming at her, he stomped upstairs, angrily slamming his bedroom door.

She had tried her best. She did what she knew was best for her child, but he would not listen, resulting in his behaviour.

She left him there in his room to cool off. Soon he became quiet and subdued.

He realised once again that his mum was right. That she always knew best. She had never failed him before, so why would she start now?

Slowly the tears stopped. The feeling of helplessness vanished. Once again, he would succumb to her will, for he knew she loved him more than that.

For there is no more.

82

The air was ripe with sunshine and smells. Smells of home drifted through the open door. What memories it invoked in the old man as he sat under the ancient elm tree in his garden.

'Ah yes, I remember my mother on her baking day as if it were yesterday.'

Memories of his boyhood flooded through his longing. Thoughts of all that had been. With a contented sigh, he puffed on his pipe.

Next thing, in a flash, he is once again that little boy with short trousers, a cap and a tie, longing for it to be teatime. How easy and simple were his delights.

'Was life really that simple?' he puzzled. 'Am I looking at it through rose-coloured glasses? Am I living in a delusion, a dream that all my yesterdays were filled with sunshine and roses?'

His mind took a leap forward, a return to the now. Once, life was good. Or was it that life then was so simple? Fewer demands, less competition?

He sighed again and smiled to himself. He was glad that he was old, glad that his life was run at a slower pace.

'Any regrets?' his conscience asked.

'Yes, only one, and it is that I never said please and thank you enough for taking all for granted, all that was given with love.'

83

The day was just beginning. Dawn had coloured the sky with a richness that words cannot adequately describe. Birds stirred, shaking their feathers to greet this, the sunniest of days.

In the village, other creatures and humans were beginning to rouse themselves.

Throwing back the bedding and grabbing her dressing gown, she made her weary way to the kitchen as she had done forever and a day. The habits of what seemed like a lifetime are hard to break.

Boiling the water. Laying the table. A ritual she had done since the day she got married.

Married! Where had the years gone?

She slipped into a kind of reverie, remembering when.

Was it so long ago? How the mind plays tricks. How we forget that time is precious. That each day we are given is special and not to be wasted on 'might have been'.

So, greet this day as if it was your last one. Never mind if the sun is not shining. Let it shine in your heart for all to see.

84

BE bold, be brave, and be constant. Be the best you can be, for the Lord your God asks for nothing more.

WHEN fear, loneliness and problems begin to smother you, when they become so large that they become bigger than you, release them to the Lord. You were not meant to walk the road alone. Ask for help. Be not proud, for in asking for help, you will become strong.

RELY not on others for your happiness. Happiness is that state of mind that comes from within and comes from contentment of the soul.

WHEN adversity befalls you, hold your breath for just one moment. React not hastily. Give your mind that split second to control your thoughts and movement. In doing so, you will be the braver, the leader of men.

GO and seek out others who are not like you. Befriend the homeless, the down and outs. Convert them not into your way of thinking but go and learn from them.

WHEN good times come your way, when all is sunshine and laughter, when sunshine fills your days, go and seek the Lord. Ask why you are so blessed, and when you hear the reply, rejoice and know you are beloved.

WHEN doom and gloom pervade your being, when your heart is heavy, seek the Lord and ask why. When you know the answer, rejoice and know you are beloved and worthy of a great lesson.

RELAX and just be, for in being, you are whole.

TO learn a truth greater than you have ever learnt before is to touch the stars.

85

With LOVE in your heart, the world is yours.

With a SMILE on your face, the world is yours.

With GRACE and prestige that comes from a confidence that all is well in your world, no one can harm you.

The light that shines from you (the light that only others see) is a reflection of the light of God.

We all know who we love being with. We all know of someone who only has to say the word 'hello', and you know that your day has become brighter.

With LOVE in our hearts, the world is brighter.

A LOVE that is shared makes the world brighter.

With a SMILE in our eyes, we see the light that shines in the world.

Go, see the light. Catch that beam. Dance in the beam for all to see.

Shine your LIGHT. Go, seek out others who are in darkness.

Share your LIGHT. Let's make this our signature tune. For knowing the song and singing the tune, let's make sure we all know the chorus, even though some may only know how to hum it.

86

'Go away', said the lady in her haste. 'Go away and leave me alone. Why pester such an old lady with your pleas of poverty and hopelessness?'

Shutting the door and returning to her chair, she began dozing. She drifted off into the blue yonder, not caring and feeling warm and mellow.

Her dream led her to a place of such beauty and bliss that she thought she had died and gone to heaven.

Slowly she came back to reality and continued with her daily doings.

When evening came, when her time for retiring came, she hoped to relive her past dream.

But this was not to be, for in her sleep state, she visited a dark, dense and unwelcoming place. Oh, how she longed to escape, but she was being held there by a force much stronger than her soul could contain.

Flashes of grotesque figures appeared before her, smiling, grimacing, and gesturing but all with hate in their eyes.

'Please stop. Please go away. Go back to where you came from. Someone, please help me.'

Morning appeared. The long night was over. Gladly she got out of bed, glad to see the sunlight.

'What, and why?' Invaded her consciousness. 'Must have been something I ate' was her conclusion from the last night's event.

It is so easy to dismiss our wild imaginings. Do we only choose to see what brings us warmth and pleasure? Why do you continually make excuses for the horrors of this world?

Wake up and see the injustices that are being perpetrated in your world. Forget the excuses that bring comfort to your feeble minds. See for yourself that you are deluding the probabilities of what is there right in front of your eyes.

I beg and beseech you, awake and see all that appears before you.

Excuses are only the comfort of the blind and weak. Injustice is the nightmare of the oppressed. Awake and see with eyes wide open. Then and only then can you sleep easily at night.

87

You may believe or not. You may wish to disregard my message as some tomfoolery, some rambling idiot that has lost his marbles. But do not judge me too hastily until you have weighed up all the angles to my cause.

There once was a lady. She was a great lady of such beauty and renown that all who cast their eyes on her fell in love with her. Suitors came from far and wide to win her favour, for she was the daughter of a rich and wise king.

Many tasks were set before these suitors, but all had failed. All had returned home. All had failed to win their prize.

By all accounts, the lady in question became bored by the continual flow of suitors. She cared little if she ever got married.

One day, while out riding, she came across a fallen deer badly injured by some poacher's arrow. Stopping to help this beautiful creature, it began talking to her in her own language.

'Leave your father's house. Sell all that belongs to you and give away what you cannot sell to the poor and needy.'

'But what of my wants?' she replied.

'You have all that you need. Go. I repeat, go and give all that you possess to the poor and needy.'

'And then what? What is there for me?'

'There is joy in knowing that my needs have been met.'

'Your needs? But who are you? A person in disguise?'

'I am your conscience. I am that part of you that

lies deep within your soul. That part that longs to be free from its shackles of possession.'

Is this not your belief too? Is this not what the world needs? We do not ask you to give more than you can comfortably afford, but it is in the giving that the soul is freed.

How much can you afford to give? Or how much can you afford not to give?

88

It was winter. Cold, frosty and bleak. She sat huddled around her fire, admiring the beautiful winter scene outside in her garden.

Picture this, a frosty morning with the sun glistening on the rooftops, the air still and quiet, but where were the birds? She had fed them. She expected a sudden rush of hungry starlings to break the silence with their noisy twittering, but no, they were gone. But where?

Where do the birds go when they have been fed and watered by your garden? Do they seek out others who care for their welfare? They do not have homes the like ours, so where do they go, and where do they fly to?

This may seem like a meaningless puzzle but stop a while and consider this for just a moment.

Where do all the people go? Those that have no homes, those that choose to travel without the freedom of possessions. Does it ever bother you that perhaps they struggle with responsibilities?

Do you ever envy them because they have no responsibilities? Freedom is such an emotive word. What does freedom mean to you?

'No cares, no worries, no ties of family or friends – heaven', I hear you cry. Is that the truth? Is that what your heart says, or is it your head speaking?

Solitude is just as heady as in the word freedom, ok in small doses, but is this how we were meant to live our lives? Is your life so balanced as to have never realised just how lucky you are? The belief that most people have is that to be 'out of sight is to be out of mind'.

People seeking the open road live each day as if it were their last. To them, each day, with its trials and tribulations, is likening to a battle that needs to be fought. But then the sweet victory, when the day is done, and they can lay themselves down to sleep in a box or a bed.

Envy not their freedom. Envy not their solitude, for theirs is the harder battle of life, for it is you that lacks the courage of a true life.

They will return, they are always with us, but it is their choice if and where they return.

89

'Happy days are here again', I hear you sing.

What is happiness? Can you explain it to someone who has never experienced happiness?

What words would you choose? That warm glow you feel? That light, bubbly feeling you feel inside? That smile? That light in your eyes for all to see?

What colour is happiness? Blue to some, gold to others. Where does happiness come from?

What a good question! Have you ever considered the answer?

Is it because it's payday? That the sun is shining, or that your baby has said its first word?

Feelings come and go. We float on this tide of emotions without a care, not conscious of the whys and wherefores of what is happening to us.

By just being in the moment, that perfect space in any given time, the reality of which we are not conscious of, it goes deeply into our subconscious state of bliss that words do not adequately describe.

Do I go too deep for you? Does not your reality of this concept ever penetrate your thoughts? Ah, bliss. Ignorance is truly bliss.

I do not criticise. I seek not to judge. But, my dears, my children, dream on, for you have nothing to trouble you.

Blessed is he that sees the funny side of life.

I sound glib. Never!

Happiness is only the other side of the coin. Relax. Be happy, for there are many more such days to come. If not, let's pretend.

156

90

Go down, go deep down to that place where you dwell. Where the real you lives and not the one that the world sees.

I dare you. I dare you to do so. The door you have slammed shut so tightly that only the mighty Archangels dare to open.

What are you ashamed of? What secrets dare you not retrieve from the dark recesses of your mind?

What are you afraid of? What demons dwell there?

They may not be of your making. They may have been put there because you were not brave enough to defend yourself.

But I am brave enough to stand by you when you release them. I am there to see that no harm befalls you. I am there to grant, to give you, all the strength that you will ever need to justify their release.

Do you not believe me? You shy away. Is it fear that pervades you? Is it embarrassment? Do the cares of others take precedence over your fears?

What if that is so? Are you so small in stature to others? Are you so insignificant as to believe in the worthlessness of your existence? Be ashamed if that is so.

I demand of you that you stand tall. Stand so tall that others lurk in your shadow. You were meant to be so.

I shout this out to you in my despair as an adoring parent. I cajole. I plead, I sympathise, I love.

Take my hand. It is very large. Rest in my arms. They are strong. I give you my strength to open that door, but you must first turn the key.

I wait patiently.

91

The little girl skipped along the road. She was happy, for today was her birthday.

Many cards had been sent to her. Her mother had read the names of the people who wished her a happy day.

'I am so lucky. So lucky to be loved by so many people', thought the little girl.

Presents, too, had surrounded her bedroom. So many she could not count them, but mummy did.

'Why do people like me?' she thought. 'What is so special about me? Why, I am not even pretty. Not like my friend, Emily, with her long blond hair and her daddy's big car.'

Simple questions deserve simple answers.

Is your perception of life so? Do you see yourself as undeserving as Mary?

Why is that so? Are you any less deserving of appreciation than the most desired of creatures?

Look and see. Look to your garden. Flowers as exotic as a lily. Flowers as small as a daisy. Why compare? Why judge one over another?

What of colour? What of perfume? Is not the sight of the first snowdrop a most welcoming sight after the long dark winter? Do we not appreciate its tenacity to brave the cold and dark days of the early months? It heralds a new and glorious rebirth of a new year. It has its place. It brings as much pleasure to us as the sweet-smelling rose.

Each flower that grows has its season. Each has its time of being. No flower is any lesser for being small. Each is as appreciated as the rest.

In God's Garden, there are many such flowers, and he loves them all.

92

DOORS. Let's consider doors. We have front doors – splendour in their appearance. We have back doors – plain but functional.

Doors we take for granted. Doors are always there. Not a riveting subject for discussion, you may think. But let's look at the symbolism here.

Walk through any door, and you enter into the future.

We begin at school. That big door that seemed so enormous when we were small but so small when we eventually close it behind us when we leave.

Yet another door has to be opened in life when we seek work, our place of employment. Yet another door must be opened, and so on, until we close the door on our own life.

Are you afraid to open that last door, the door that leads you on to your next life?

'What is behind that door?' you may ask, afraid to imagine.

Do not be. Wonder and adventures await you. The door that you now hate, the door that seems a barrier, is not the dreadful barrier that pervades your nightmares. It is merely the door to your next existence. The one you entered through when you were first born.

You have already been through this door. You will recognise it when you see it, not with fear but with gentle knowing. Perhaps you welcome it, and perhaps fear will no longer be with you.

The door holds no barrier. The door welcomes you. You are expected.

Do not fear the door, for friends wait on the other side.

93

Down the road she wandered, lost in her dreaming. Gone was the problem that had pervaded her thoughts, gone at last the sleepless night, the constant badgering of her mother.

'Shame,' she thought, 'that it had to end like this'. But there had been little choice. It was not the way she would have been chosen. So be it.

Relationships are difficult. They are the hardest tests we are given. We cannot run away from them no matter how hard we try.

To have power over another, to know that you have that power, can become your master. It is so easy to become that bully. Power can be a heady concoction. Fear is its sidekick but let that be. We seek another solution.

Relationships are our test in the pursuit of happiness. Happiness, in all its wonder and glory, is the goal we all seek. Do not deceive yourself into believing any other.

Where do we go to resolve such problems? A counsellor, perhaps? A local priest? A true and trusted friend?

Believe in yourself. Believe in that little voice that comes to you in your darkest hour, but how often do we stop to listen? Do we ever trust what we hear?

You have such a knowing. Such knowledge has been programmed into you if only you would stop, look, and listen.

Next time you have a problem, and before you

react with your usual haste and judgement, stop, look, and listen to that inner voice, for it knows the future. It knows that what is about to be said is not the real you. The real you is wise and caring. So please, for all concerned, love and judge not, for ye are to be judged.

94

As she sat listening to her favourite music, time for her was at a stand-still. Slipping slowly into the rhythm of the music, she drifted far away onto a different level.

'Bliss', she thought. 'Nothing is wrong. All is well in my world.'

She was not sure how long she had been in her daydreaming. No matter. Time was hers. No rush or demands, and yet why did she feel guilty?

Lazy was the first word that came to mind.

'You lazy lump. Nothing better to do?' She sighed, yawned and stretched. 'So what. Time is mine. I have all the time in the world. My life can wait. I'll put it on hold just for today.'

Is your life on hold, and if so, what are you waiting for?

Go and do it now. Go and live today as if there was no tomorrow.

Dreams can come true if you let them happen. If you would only plan for them to happen.

Go and plan that holiday. Go and change your job. Move house. Sign up for a course.

Life is all about living it. LIVING in big capital letters.

Why wait? What are you waiting for? Lazy or scared? I know what I'd rather be called, and it's neither of these two.

95

School days are supposed to be the happiest times of your life. Were they for you? Or were they the most painful? Life is not easy. Life was not meant to be so.

When we were children, that dreaded time of school, that prison that swallowed us up, a necessary evil, you may say, a just and worthy cause?

But take it back even further to when, as a baby, from the first time we took a breath, we had to learn how to make our presence known. And so it continued. Likewise, as of now, even in our dotage, the lessons go on and on.

When do we come to a time when all our lessons are learned? When we are dead? When we cease to even want to live anymore?

The mind, in its infinite wisdom, is an amazing concept. Its function is to expand, to grow without thought of reasoning. To be seen to stop growing is a sign of infirmity. (I ramble on.)

Are the lessons we learn solely for our benefit? Does life improve if we learn our lessons well and with some haste?

What happens when we make the same mistake over and over again? When we stubbornly refuse to learn the lessons the first time around?

It is a very wise man indeed that knows the difference between judging what our needs are, for the ego is that monster that must be fought and won over.

I do not judge you. I do not seek to show you the

way, for no one can do so for you. I only illustrate and draw attention to you who struggle so. Because of your obstinacy, your inflated egos, your darn right determination never to improve, never to learn yet again, the lessons set before you. Instead, you choose to build that brick wall higher and higher until it blocks out all the light and all the chances of ever seeing over the top of it.

Why do you do it? Is it because your ego knows better? Never mind how many times you need to put a plaster on that sore knee after a fall. Is that wall so comforting? Is it a symbol of what needs to be done, not today, but maybe someday?

My lecture is over, and my speaking is done. I have but one question. Why do you choose the rough and stony path when there is another way?

Knock down that brick wall, for sweet rolling green meadows await you.

96

Have you been shopping today? Has your day been filled with all the demands that a family and running a household brings?

Many demands are made on our time. Is that of our choosing? Is this what life is all about?

We all have needs. People have needs. Many might say that too many demands are made of our time.

How we spend time is interesting, do you not think so?

What is a pleasure to some is a chore to another. Take shopping as an example. If you live alone, shopping could be your only contact with another human being. A place of escapism, with warmth and connection. A purpose in your daily life of non-existence. To others, it is the last place they would rather be.

And yet, we are creatures of habit. Routine is the necessary evil that pervades our lives (time for bed, time to eat, work, etc.)

What happens when our daily routine is broken? The unexpected happens. We sleep in, we miss the bus, and the clock stops. Do we panic? Do we curse and swear? Or do we accept the change that has just occurred? The need to be stopped in our tracks, take stock and re-think our lives.

Do we take kindly to this opportunity? Do we hate change? Each of us must, at some time, realise that change can be for the best. For how do we know that there is a better life if we don't?

97

The sun was beginning to set. Glorious colours of red and gold flooded the sky. She breathed a sigh of relief, for it had been a long day. A day when many difficult decisions had to be made.

The choices that led her to make her final decision had been all too few. To swallow her pride once more, or to forgive and forget, making allowances once more, just this one more time?

She had considered long and with quiet deliberation. Her logical mind had risen once again to the surface. She would go on. She had nowhere to hide and nowhere to run to. The years that had been, the years of joint ventures, had been pleasing enough. Life could have been much worse, and with honesty, the passing years had been all she could have expected.

And the future years? Who knows our future? Perhaps plodding along in the same vein may not be so bad. She was lucky in her marriage, considering others.

But this she knew without a shadow of a doubt that from now on she, and only she, would be the strong one.

Gone were the days of being small. Gone were the days of being someone's 'put down'. She knew from this day forth a new resolve to be free and to be rid of all dependability on others.

With quiet reflection, she smiled and gave thanks, for she had learned a great lesson.

98

TOLERANCE. A difficult word. A difficult meaning. A difficult lesson for all to learn.

What does tolerance mean to you? Understanding? Patience? Unconditional love?

The dictionary gives many such meanings. We each have our own interpretations.

How do you see yourself? Tolerant or intolerant?

Difficult. I know which one we would like to be known by. Is tolerance just another ploy to undermine us? Just an irritation when we realise we are losing our patience? The neon sign that flashes in our head when we know what we really should be saying, and not the heated words of anger that flow from our mouths?

How to cultivate tolerance would be a good lesson to learn. We tell ourselves that next time we will try harder. We will be patient.

To learn tolerance is to win the argument.

Think on this when your opponent is getting heated, his voice begins to get louder, and words tumble from his mouth. Use that time to remain calm, collect your thoughts, and centre yourself.

In that moment, you are energised with your own divinity. Your one true self will emerge, and victory is yours.

99

Let's take the thought of happiness.

What lovely colour pervades our minds? Does happiness mean to you yellow with a hint of gold? The brightest blue or the deepest shade of pink?

How does happiness feel? Could you describe it to someone who has never felt it? Quite a challenge.

What does happiness mean to you? I expect your list could be endless but wait. Let's pause for a while, for we are the lucky ones.

Step outside your world, your bubble of existence. Look and see the other side of happiness.

What do we see? What do we feel? What colour is around us now?

Consider this, then. When you rise from your slumbers, even before you draw on your curtains to let in the light, what colour will you be this day?

Will it be a blue day, a black day, or a golden day? And whose colour are you going to clash with?

Perhaps your colour will blend nicely with all the other colours you will meet today.

100

There was once a little boy, tiny in stature but big in heart. His days were spent studying. Not for him, the great outdoors of football or fishing. No, his passion was learning. He never tired of reading or struggling with mathematical problems. To him, this was his world. All his needs were met in books.

One day, he was struck down with violent headaches so bad that his vision blurred.

Reading now was out of the question. Oh, how he fought his rage of disappointment. He could only hold his beloved books. In fits of despair, the books were flung across the room. For now, he began to hate them.

Until one day, lost in his daydreaming, he realised that perhaps there was another way. Another way of learning, of acquiring knowledge.

'Perhaps what I need is to experience all that I have learned of distant lands, birds, plants and famous people.'

His thoughts jumped way beyond what his young mind could ever envisage.

Do we ever consider that there is another way? A different way of looking at life, of learning, of gaining knowledge, other than the one we are familiar with? Does it always have to be the same well-trodden path of our immediate existence?

Comfortable though it may seem, how do we know if there is perhaps an easier way?

Something usually happens in our lives, something quite drastic or unforeseen, when we have no choice but to change our habits. Though we may fight and scream a little, it can be for our good if we would only give it a try.

So please remember 'a change is as good as a rest'. Without change, the world would never grow.

101

'Regrets, I've had a few. But then again, too few to mention', goes the song.

We all have regrets. We would not be normal if we did not. They say that hindsight is a wonderful thing. Indeed, it is. We all wished we were blessed by it.

As we look back on past mistakes and hasty decisions that we have made, oh, how much better should our lives be now?

But then again, who are we but mere mortals? We are here to learn all about making judgements and decisions.

With hindsight, would our lives be any better? Would life be rather boring if we were right every time?

Nobody would like us. They would see us as 'a bit of a clever dick'. 'A know-all' who was boring and brash.

No. Let's be normal. Let's make our mistakes, for we have more fun from learning from them.

Just think about it – life without regrets. We may as well live in 'cloud cuckoo land'. A dream or a nightmare?

Be truthful now!

102

CIRCLES. Let's explore circles. Let's see the symbolism here.

A circle is the continuation of a constant flow. A line in time with space in and around it. The circle of life, you may say, is a fine example. The circle of seasons is another one, and so we could go on.

What does a circle mean to you? Draw one in the air. We begin and we end right back at the beginning again.

The problem with circles is that they go nowhere. They only continue to set themselves back onto the same course again.

Life has a habit of showing us that if we do not learn the lesson the first time around, it will come back to haunt us yet again until we do.

How we long to break that cycle, the circle of repeated habit. We try to convince ourselves, to comfort ourselves with the adage of 'old habits die hard'.

I try not to be glib, for choices are always there if we only choose to learn a different way of thinking.

So, stop. Break that circle. Snap the chain that automatically takes us back to the beginning for re-entry. Find that weakest link, one that has been worn through with good intentions. See that link snap with a smile, which forms with its shape of things to come.

103

As you know, or may not know, your life at this very moment is being watched over by your guardian. By the angel who has been with you since time immemorial.

How do you feel about that? Pleased? Honoured? Troubled? Guilty?

Look, and see for yourself. Sense and feel that you are not alone. Difficult? No time? Don't believe it?

Well, maybe not yet, but come the day you need our help, we will be there.

For have you not the old habit of calling on us only in times of great distress? When you, yourself, cannot heal or help the situation?

Please remember us when good times come your way, for we are still there beside you.

Forget us not, for we are part of you as you are part of us.

Strength in numbers?

104

NOISE. Let's discuss noise. An irritation or relief? A noise as a vibration or melody?

What does noise mean to you? Let's make a list.

A bird's call, a child's laughter, church bells, and the ring at the door when the postman calls with a parcel. Wonderful and fulfilling?

But what of irritation? The constant beat of a loud vibration from next door's music. The sound of a pneumatic drill of a workman. The irritation of a dog's constant barking at night.

Each sound has its own vibration, whether it irritates or soothes. This depends not on the sound but on how you perceive it.

The ringing of a doorbell. Is that an intrusion or a welcome? This depends on our expectations or where we are in our lives.

(This could lead to so many different pathways. Let us not get bogged down with that line of thought.)

See that sound, in all its variations, is just beautiful as the rest.

Is the dawn chorus of a blackbird an irritation to some or a beautiful alarm clock to others? The expectation leads us to many different levels of evaluation.

But all who hear sounds rejoice and be blessed, for this is a reminder that you live and have been given a great blessing.

105

The sun was shining that day. It should not have been, though. His thoughts were angry, venomous.

'Ba humbug. Life. How I am sick of it. Nowt but trouble and best to rid of it. It's not worth the effort of getting up in the mornings.'

This poor sad soul, this lonely and seemingly pathetic creature, preferred the darkness and his life of bitterness. It supplied him with all the energy he needed to live.

To him, life meant challenges. It meant being polite and sympathetic to other people's needs. No time for that, not him. 'We are only here for a short time, so grab what you can with both hands.'

This does not have a happy ending. It only illustrates the other side of the coin, the side that I see of this reader's life.

Yes, you. You that are holding this book in anticipation of some glorious revelation that this other poor soul experienced.

Not so, I am sorry to say. Let this not affect you. Pity him if you feel the need. Perhaps you know of a like-minded soul. The one you try to avoid.

Pity is fine in the right place, but it can be misplaced. Perhaps next time you come amongst your lost soul, smile at his intolerance. Be patient and gentle with his abusive language. Let not your impatience rush you away from him. In your defence, rest awhile with him. Try to see him in a different light. Pretend that you are he, and he is you. For your inner knowledge, your divine spark will transform any negativity thrust at you.

Be brave. Nothing can harm you. Be my soldier.

That brave warrior who knows. You just know that somewhere amongst that grime and darkness beats a heart that longs to be like you if only someone somewhere believes it too.

106

The doll was broken. It had been an accident, and she was sorry.

'Yes, Mummy, it was me. I didn't mean to do it. It was an accident. I am sorry.'

'Never mind, dear. Accidents do happen.'

So, all was now well. Panic over, or so she thought.

Later that day, there were more problems, more tears, more woe, and more hugs of reconciliation until the long day was over.

While she slept, she dreamt. She dreamt that she was that pretty doll that had been accidentally broken that day.

She did not fear the pain. She felt no loss of being discarded. She did appreciate the tears of her loss thought.

Where was she to go now? All that remained of her was a hand full of broken pottery, no use to anyone. Could she be glued together? Could she be saved? Was she worth saving?

Choices had to be made. Decisions. A long discussion presided over her. Her that had once been whole and beautiful. Her that was once loved is now a heap of rubble.

But all was not lost. Love prevailed. Gentle hands slowly pieced her back together again.

Though her beauty had been impaired, for now she had a wonky ear and a chip missing out of her nose. Yet she did not mind, for she had survived when she thought all was lost.

With love, all had been restored.

107

It all began one sunny morning. Nothing special had been planned for that day, but fate was about to take a hand.

It all began when the car would not start. The air turned blue with Dad's cries for help. (For at the last minute, a day's outing had been planned.)

Gloom descended on the family. Fear of not going anywhere descended on the family.

Charlie was sick. The cat had diarrhoea. Mother cut her finger, and Susan burst into tears because a friend phoned with a better offer. Doom and gloom where there was once sunshine and expectations.

Life. That is what we call it. LIFE in all its big capital letters. Expectation, hopes, and fears. This is life. This is real life.

Not a complete disaster, though, in the bigger schemes of things, you may say. But sometimes, when dreaded fate (whoever he is) takes a hand, we lose our sense of who is in charge. The fact that we are in charge is but a senseless excuse because we believe we are incapable of change.

Do not blame fate. Do not see it as a separate entity from yourself. You are your own fate. Attraction is the conclusion, but not even that. The senses are but a thought away from the choices that we make.

Fate can be wonderful, if that is a word of your choosing. Fate is only another word for choice.

So, smile, and start choosing.

108

'The autumn leaves pass by my window, the autumn leaves of red and gold' goes the song. One of my favourites. Maybe one of yours too?

The song paints a picture in our minds of beauty and melancholy. Of time that is passing us by and a realisation that all too soon, things decay and die.

Perhaps relationships may die. Our memory of what has been, of regrets, of past loves and friendship, a time of 'might have beens, of what ifs?'

Are our memories our trophies, our achievements, or our regrets? Perhaps a mixture of both, and yet, would we change any of them? Perhaps some, but not all of them.

What I am trying to say is that memories, be they good or bad, are the building blocks of who and where we are in our lives.

Memories, painful sometimes but necessary, of lessons we have learned.

Bless your memories. See them for what they are. Your victories or defeats, but always your strength for things yet to come.

109

Is happiness a must for you? Is it that elusive dream that you hope one day will come true?

What will happiness bring you? A new car, a new house, the latest gadgets that you see on your TV, a new partner? I could go on.

And while you wait, why wait for this great day to dawn? What of your life now, at this very moment?

We all have dreams. That is right. Without dreams, Everest would not have been climbed, and the Berlin Wall would still stand.

But just now, this very moment in your life, where is it going? Is your life on hold until the dream materialises? As you think of an answer, remember this. Is your life any better now than if your dreams were fulfilled? Do we not replace them with another until we are satisfied?

Contentment can be just as elusive as your dreams.

Why do you do so? Is your life so bad, so filled with grief that only tomorrow keeps you hanging on?

Hold tight. Please hold tight to dismiss that thought, for what happens if tomorrow never comes? Just think about what you have missed along the way.

110

(From a grieving soul who is sorry for the pain and grief that I caused when I walked the Earth-plane, this is my confession. Read and believe.)

I call on you to stop reading this book. Put it down for a moment to explore all that has gone before. Where are you in your belief system?

Is it all making sense to you now? Understand what we are teaching you and trying to show you the error of your way.

Be not angry or troubled by these words. The realisation that this is not just any ordinary book, but a book of a great truth that we on this side of the veil shout out to you for all to hear.

We send you our love, and our deepest respect, for we do know and understand the troubles of your world. They were once ours.

We have a sense of duty to be of assistance. Let us not fail. I seek not to alarm you with these words. I haste not in my temper. I try to cool my heels, but oh, my dear ones, how I long to ease your burdens by my example. (I ramble on, please forgive me, but I do so with a loving heart.)

PLEASE, in capital letters. Please, wake up, for time is not on your side, dear reader. 'Love one another as I love you.' This is not only the quotation of a mad fool but of an obscure mind that lurks in the ethos. I am real. As real as you who sit and read my words. Please take on board this simple message of one who knows a great truth, who has been there and suffered because he would not listen and who wasted his life through neglect.

I pray for you. I bleed for you. How I long to put right the wrongs when I had the chance to do so.

This is why I speak now. Heed my words: 'Love one another as I love you', for love is all there is. Love will see us through.

As the darkness that man creates, be that beacon of light. The world needs you. I need you to do this for me, as one lost soul to maybe another. I doubt it, for you would not have chosen to read this book.

I'll leave you now. My message has been spoken. I leave the destiny of the world in your hands. Love her. Love all who walk on her soil. Without love, we are nothing, and all of mankind is lost.

111

Miriam's Story

I love flowers. Do you have a favourite? They say you can see the whole world in the head of a flower.

Flowers are special. Each flower has its own smell, and the perfume of your favourite flower is second to none.

When I was young, I collected flowers. I dried and pressed them, then placed them in my keepsake book. Each one was dated, and where it had been found was neatly written on the page. How I loved my book. It was a keepsake, a treasured memory of places visited and of long hot sunny days when I was young.

There came a time when I could not see very well. Nor could I travel very far, so my poor collection of flowers ceased. Oh, how I longed to travel, maybe to other lands to add to my collection, but I could only dream.

Many people brought me coloured books of different flowers, but little did they realise it was not the same as picking that flower, holding that flower, and smelling that flower. Not the same. Indeed, very superficial, but they thought they were being kind.

Life can be like that. We see pictures in books of people, places, and stories we would like to be part of. So what are you waiting for? Make it happen. Do not leave it too late, for there is nothing like the real thing. Nothing like holding, caressing and smelling your dream. Nothing like the real thing.

112

Is it the end of the day? How has your day been? Full of sunshine and smiles? Or tears and black clouds? Do you go to bed with a heavy heart or full of expectations?

Ponder awhile on the day's events. Where was your intention to be who you are and not what others expect of you?

Problems arise, that is so. Solutions arise, but not always. We deem ourselves very lucky if they do, so where do we go from here? Judging by your mood, not far, for all is well. Or the furthest away we can get?

Remedies. Ah, yes, remedies. The answer to all prayers. This is where we must dig deep into the well of knowledge, that book of inspiration, to turn our lives around.

Who owns this book? You or him upstairs? A partnership, perhaps? Believe in yourself, for you are the procreator of all things.

You are that divine spark seeking to be on the same level as the gods themselves. And why not? Are you not made in his image? Are you not blessed with the wisdom of Saul?

Demean not yourselves, for you are as great a creation as the king who rules your lands.

Problems are but stepping-stones along the way, frustrating but glorious when solved.

So go and be your own trouble-shooter. See and believe. For you are victorious. Believe no other.

113

Martha's Story

When the seed is ripe, it will flourish and grow, this you would agree? But let the seed be dry and wizen, and then all life has been extinguished.

To watch a seed grow is simply a miracle, do you not agree? The life force that is contained in a tiny speck is beyond our comprehension but, believe we must.

Nature is complex. Nature is wise. She knows that in all things, life is a continual cycle that never ceases.

Your daily routine is likened to that cycle. You get up, eat, work, eat, and then sleep, just as the seasons. Just as that seed that ripens, dies and is reborn again in the spring.

Does the wonder of it ever cease to amaze you? Or do you, like many, take it all for granted? The unseen forces, the divas that work without your knowledge, you give it not a second thought that your flowers will automatically bloom once again.

How does it know that little seed when it's time to germinate? How does it know that it is spring and time to flourish? Is there some unseen vibration, some great divine energy that is linked with the sun, the rain and the stars?

I do not intend to make heavy weather of it, but nature in all its glory is a force and unspoken chain that for aeons of years has been your survival mechanism, for you are part of it.

Look and see with new eyes. Look and see but do not judge for you judge yourself.

And the seed that is dry, why it is dead through lack of nourishment, love and hope.

114

Rebecca's Story

As the days grow longer and winter is upon us, do not see long gloomy days of darkness. Fail not to see the need for sleep and quiet days in your abode. The sunshine that seemed to fill your days in the spring and summer lends itself to a time of quiet reflection. For does not nature in her wisdom see animals, birds, seedlings, and vegetation wither and die while others sleep or find their way to distant sunnier shores?

Be ye not sad. Instead, be thankful that your days are shorter and that it is now time for your body to lose some of its energy for 'doing'.

You may fight it and choose to live abroad in the sunshine. So be it. But nature knows. Nature will not be duped. For if we choose to live by the sun, the body reaps its own rewards.

All through our lives, the internal clock that we see and feel drives us ever onward. To what?

A time when the springs break? Times when we are too tired to wind up the clock and fear a breakdown? That fear that time is running out for us, for we have so much yet to do. So many other things need our attention. We dare not unwind for fear of never restarting.

Why do you panic so? Nature knows. Nature knows only too well that in the spring, after a long sleep, all is reborn, and all will blossom again. For the sun awakens us. The sun smiles down on us, and we blossom.

115

Thomas's Story

I once had a dog. He was brave and a wonderful friend. We would go roaming, Ben and me. Oh, how we would run and play fight. We had fun, and my days were full of happy times. But then I grew up and had no time for Ben. Other pursuits filled my days.

Ben grew lazy and old. He would look at me with sad eyes, hoping that maybe we could go roaming like we used to.

I loved him still, even though I did neglect him. One day suddenly, he died. Grief, like I never knew before, engulfed me and filled me with shock and disbelief. My friend was no more.

It is at times like this that we trip down memory lane remembering all that has been and now can never be repeated.

Are we the better for such an occasion? Is the pain of losing a loved one a lesson of our own mortality?

This can never be. This can and will only seek to re-adjust our own mortality into the realisation that rather it be a joy or a dread, nothing lasts, and nothing should be taken for granted.

I shout this out to you. You, like me, took all for granted that nothing would change. But things must change. Change is inevitable. It is progress. The world and mankind progress. But we think it's not for us. We are not involved. It only happens to other people.

But you are that other person, do you not see it?

You are the other person to the other person!

My words I write in haste, for time is short, and the need to share is great.

I plead I beg, let all your thoughts of inevitability be lost. Let new and divine thoughts filter through. Believe now, believe my way, for my lesson is …? Or have you worked it out for yourself and need no reminder?

116

Abigail's story

Go down. Go down this very minute to a place of your choice in meditation. Be it a beach, a rocky cave, a rolling plateau, or a tropical jungle. Go to where you feel safe, warm and cared for. A place of beauty, of coming home to where your heart longs to be.

Once you are there, rest awhile, look and see everything about you. Are there animals there? Are there flowers, colours, or people even?

'And why?' you may ask, 'should this picture have been specially prepared for me? Who or why was I put into this picture?'

Do you not know? Do you really not know, or do you doubt the very existence of your soul's longings? It longs to bring that inner peace, that peace that you know is there (for have you not been told so?) if only you had the courage and patience to seek it. 'Not for me, not for me. Don't believe. Not possible.'

I come to say to you all that are burdened and heavy laden, to rest awhile. To stop the fight that you have with your inside voice, for does it not speak softly to you? Do you not get that little glimmer of a whisper in your moments of quiet solitude?

What demons do you think lurk there? Be at peace, for there is much to gain, much beauty, much contentment there, the like of which you could not imagine.

So please, my friend, I speak of one who knows,

my friend, share with me the treasures of your abundance.

Peace be with you.

117

Problems, what are they? Lessons that we need to learn? A situation that we have created, be it through our own stupidity or the intervention of others?

To wrestle with a problem, large or small, only seeks to frustrate our thoughts. Oh, how the mind seeks and enjoys wrestling with the answer.

To leave well alone and let the solution rise to the surface would be to have the wisdom of Solomon. But we know only too well that when we are in the middle of a problem, we are in a constant state of flux.

We say, 'Sleep on it'. We say, 'Tomorrow is another day'. That is good advice if only we take it. It is so easy to say than to do.

But bless your problems. See them as an opportunity to grow. Do not expect it to be easy, for regrets are our building blocks for a new tomorrow and the inevitability that only seeks to free us from our egos.

118

Samuel's Story

How many times a day do you stop and think of others in your life besides yourself? Once, twice, or even more?

Does this depend on your mood or even choosing to be with people? Stop and count this very day. I give you a test. See if you can count the good with the bad. All are important.

Why the test?

I bring to your notice just how important you are when you are amongst society. Your very thoughts and demeanour shine through, and your very essence links you to others. You are a powerful being. Fail not to see the importance of your existence. No one goes unnoticed.

So, my challenge to you today is to be conscious of your thoughts and attitude, for you can do much damage or good. Which is it to be?

119

Sheila's Story

When I was young, I had a dream that one day, I would travel to distant shores. Many books I had read on the subject, and many a night I would lay awake dreaming of such places.

To ride on a camel. To canoe down some exotic river listening to all the animals in some distant jungle. To see pyramids and mountains covered in snow. I could go on.

As I grew older, life for me took a different turn. I had not realised we were poor so that my dreams of travelling were not to be.

But fate had other things in store for me.

The war, the 'great war' as you called it, happened. I was to meet a man, an old and learned gentleman who needed an assistant to be his companion and secretary. His booking-agent-come-organiser. This was just the opportunity I had longed for. Fate, indeed, was kind to me. My dreams were to be fulfilled, or so I thought. Fate can also be cruel, just as if, by a twist of fate, the war began.

Travel ceased to be an option, resources were scarce, and manpower was needed elsewhere. Industry was where I ended up working, in the dirt and grime when my soul cried for sunshine and distant lands.

The realisation came to me later.

It's not for me. It's not for me to judge fate. For who am I, a grain of sand, a small cog in a large wheel, or a mighty being whose orders are acted upon without question?

To do one's duty and to fight through disappointment is, and must be, the crown of thorns that we all bear. Duty or not, disappointment, heartbreaking cliches, they are all necessary, for does it not make us realise that all dreams may not come true?

But hope, that glorious feeling of energy that we cling onto when we are bogged down with duty. With hope in our hearts, aye in our very being, gives us the courage to go on.

I hope my little story sees you through your 'times of duty'. Perhaps one day, who knows?

Fate does.

120

Marth'a Story

When I was a little girl, I had many dolls. Big ones, tiny little ones, mama dolls, and baby dolls that closed their eyes when you laid them down. They each had a name. Many were named after flowers, for I loved flowers as much as my dolls.

Each one was special and had her place in my family. Many were dressed in fashionable clothes, hats, gloves and shoes, all they needed. I took turns with them when I slept at night time. Each one would be dressed in her nightie, snuggled, cuddled and kissed goodnight.

They were my substitute family, for I had no brothers or sisters. Mother was always too busy with Papa – well, he worked away. Nanny and me, she was all I needed, plus my dolls.

To live in this dream world would seem idyllic, but we should not substitute and never make excuses if real life is too harsh. To make the excuse, to pretend that all is well, that the involvement of others is too much for us, there we only fool ourselves.

Courage is not about seeming to be brave, not in the literal sense, but 'going out on a limb', going outside your comfort zone, being that little bit scared of touching other people, those that we find uncomfortable. Stretching yourself not in a condescending way (for you may need the help of others).

We look, read, sympathise, donate, and think that is all that is needed. Not so. Not enough. Go give your time, your love, and your very being to that place, touching, talking with them, and then your soul grows. Then you are worthy of being a candidate for your golden crown.

I see you hesitate all too much. Consider this then, did not your master Jesus say unto you, 'I leave the world in your hands, for I can do no more?'

It's now up to you. Be brave. Find the time. No excuses.

121

When your day is going badly. When the heaviness of your burden drags you so low that you think, 'all is lost. I will never get through this. It's all too much I cannot go on. Enough is enough.'

Stop and step aside from your despair. Put down all thoughts of hopelessness. This is not too big a thing for you to carry. For nothing is given to you that is too much for you to bear. It may seem that no one carries such a burden in the entire world, but they do.

Despair, in all its blackness and heaviness, only seeks for you to stop, slow down and seek help. For to carry such a load is the testing of your own stubbornness if you do not.

This may sound glib. Forgive me if I anger you, but in despair, we do not see clearly.

I only seek to readjust and help you come to a different thought form. For when in times of great need, let go of the ego. Let go and let in the light of God, for he indeed waits for your call.

122

Sylvia's Story

When I was young, in my late teens, I loved a boy very much, and he loved me. We made a vow one day to marry, settle down and raise kids, just like people do.

One day he went away. He needed to find a job, for work around here was scarce.

We said our goodbyes, not knowing when we would see each other again. The days were long and the nights even longer.

Days passed. They turned into months, then a year, then two years. He did write but not very often. Oh, how I missed him. Still, I understood it was necessary.

The golden day came when he returned. Oh, my dears, how he had changed. Gone were his good looks and his smile. The light had gone out of him.

Sorry, I was so sorry. So ashamed that I expected so much of this wonderful human being. Guilt filled my heart and mind. I didn't mean for this to happen.

'Forgive me' was all I could say to him.

But my story must be told, for the ending is indeed happy. We are man and wife now. But the moral I do now reiterate. Expectations, we all have them. It is the expectation of others that destroys our self-image.

123

PERSEVERANCE – a rather profound and noble word.

Perseverance was the watchword that was written on many a school report at the end of a long term.

Perseverance. How well does that sit with you? A word your mother used? A warning that was given to you by your teacher and mentor? That dreaded word that still haunts our childhood memories?

Does the word perseverance now have a different connotation? Do you see it as a glorified rebuke to lesser fledglings? Did we ever learn the lesson of 'perseverance?'

As we grow older, we realise that to persevere is something we have done all our lives. And where has it got us?

Where indeed. Are we any better for persevering with problems of learning or of mastering the art of relationships? I like to think that we are.

To persevere is to dedicate ourselves to progress, to that final peak in whatever task we have set ourselves. You can congratulate yourself on a great achievement but do not chide yourself if victory is still out of reach.

Perseverance teaches us patience. It teaches us dedication. Not an easy concept for most. But to the few? Well, they ride high on a cloud of self-glory, and so they should. For to persevere is to dedicate yourself to a calling of the soul.

Stop and listen sometimes. Stop and rest awhile when the going gets tough. Stop, and reach out for the highest pinnacle. There is no rush, haste, or speed on who can get there first.

It's the getting there. It's the journeying, and it's knowing that someday, very soon, the glory is to be all yours.

124

As we journey along life's pathway, judging others whether we have cause to or not, take a look around you. What do you see?

'Nothing special,' you may say, 'everything is ordinary, just as it should be.'

Is it? Is it really? Or is it that our perception of normality is so mundane that we never see beyond what is staring at us? It's what we don't see.

It's that crack of light that shines on a piece of broken glass. A yellow weed that has pushed itself through the dirt and grime. That bird call that struggles to hear itself over the noise of traffic. Nature knows. She battles against humans. She does her best to show us the alternative.

City life is hard. Hard on the patience of man. It is that necessary evil in our lives. It is called 'city living'. The scourge of the many. It is a necessary commodity that only seeks to dull our senses.

But I ask you all who dwell in the city to see beyond what nature has to offer. Weeds that grow into flowers amongst the cracks in the pavement. The wildlife that strays into your gardens at night. Much has been documented about such creatures. Does that not tell you something? Does that not awaken you to another existence?

Work in the city is necessary, but so is the contrast to that existence.

'No problem, we cope', you say.

My meaning is simple. My contradiction, I explain.

Co-existence in all forms leads us to a place of patience, of that belief that to cope with the pressures it brings only seek to annihilate our piece of mind.

So, can you not see the gist of my story? Whether I ramble or speak your belief system, it is of your choosing.

But please have patience. See beyond the obvious, for beauty in all its simplicity awaits you.

125

Today is a good day, is it not? The sun is shining, and the birds are singing. All is well with the world. At least all is well in your world, is it not?

Pause a while and consider this question. Do not compare your world with your neighbour, for they live in a different time zone to you.

I see you hesitate. Why for? Is your life so bad, so grim that to change would be the answer to your prayers? You do yourself no favours if you do so, for change is all about what you can do for yourself. You need no other to do that for you.

Consider this, then. Why have you not done so already? What are you waiting for? Nobody else can do it for you. Be brave, my little friend, be brave. Test the elements. You will be surprised. You will be amazed at what is out there.

Many books have been written on the subject. I expect you have read a few. It all sounded so good, so plausible. A big yes was given when you read those wise words. But the 'words of the wise' on paper seemed to you then plausible. They made it sound so easy. So, if that is the case, what are you waiting for?

A challenge. I set you a challenge. Go and do just one thing out of the ordinary. Go out with pride and courage. Be that brave warrior who treads on unknown land. Take your courage in your hands. Sign on for that course, and book that singles holiday. Leave all others behind with wonder and awe at the sudden change in you. You can do it. What are you waiting for?

The victory is yours. For who knows where the first step will lead you?

126

Fredrick's Story

I am tall. Not as tall as you who writes this, but large enough to be spotted in a crowd. Mother was tall. Father was even taller. Size matters, or so I was told.

All through my childhood, fun and finger-pointing played a big part. I learned to ignore the perpetrators, believing that my size would not matter one day and that I would become the norm.

Have you a disability? A distinguishing mark? Any sign of an infirmity? How do you cope? Do you only go out at night or wear darkened sunglasses in the middle of winter? Or do you brave the stares, believing in your own worth?

In many ways, we are the lucky ones. Our infirmity is visible. Beware the person who is deformed in their hearts, for they leave a scar.

We had no control. Theirs is of their own choosing.

127

Have you ever owned a pet? It does not matter how big or small, be it a furry or feathered friend. I call them friends because that is what they are.

I once had a friend. His name was, well, that's not important at this time. Let's say his name was the name of a flower. Strange name for a dog, especially a male dog, you may think, but all will be explained later.

I had a birthday not long ago. Money was given to me by my Aunt Bessie. What to do with it was a big question. A big decision had to be made on how I would spend it.

'Impatience' was my middle name. Saving it was not an option, so with birthday money 'burning a hole in my pocket', Mother and I set out on a spending spree.

By chance, Mother spotted her friend taking her dog to the vet. It had a bad tooth and so would not eat. We offered to accompany her, as much catching up on gossip as needed.

Then I saw him. Oh, how my heart jumped a beat. This is what I had been looking for. A friend to call my very own. It was love at first sight.

Mother saw my face. She knew right there and then where my birthday money was going. (For this poor wee mite had been lost, then taken to the vets to be re-housed.)

Poppy. I decided to call him Poppy. It summed up how I felt about him, for they are survivors. They spring up in the most unexpected places. They come in all shades, and we are always grateful for the colour they bring into our lives.

128

Elizabeth's Story

There once was a little boy. He had a secret. A big secret that he kept to himself. He dared not share it with another.

As the years passed, his big secret slowly slipped away from the necessity to share it. It simply ceased to exist, until one day, just by chance, he picked up a leaflet that lay blowing in the gutter.

It read, 'Roll up and see the magician. Mr Blotto is here to entertain you.'

'Sounds fun', he thought. 'I'm going.'

An interesting evening ensued. It was fun. At least, he thought so until a volunteer was needed from the audience.

He was picked. To his horror, the spotlight fell on him. They clapped him onto the stage. Feeling very foolish, he picked out a playing card. Relaying it to memory, he placed it back into the pack. The act continued until he was to be hypnotised. Horror! 'No, please no,' was his cry. Too late. There was no escape.

All he could remember was a voice somewhere above him, far away in the distance, calling his name. He was not playing this game. He resented making a fool of himself, and it had to stop.

Suddenly it all changed. No longer was there an element of resentment. He remembered his long dark secret that had lain dormant for all these years.

Yes. I know now. I release it to the world. I cannot be blamed now, for I am not in control. He shouted out aloud to all that would hear.

'Listen to me. I now share my secret with you all. I seek not to deceive. Go back to the beginning and see for yourself that all you have to do to prove yourself worthy is to love and be loved. Then nothing can harm you.'

At this, a cheer broke out. For now, he was 'wide awake'.

129

Bethany's Story

God is love. God sees all, God knows all.

Jesus gave his life for us. We give ours to others.

To be of service to God is our greatest love.

To give service to our fellow man is as great a love that can ever be written.

To give of ourselves, why God asks no more of us.

To give our time, our love or energy, why we do the service as would an angel.

Be of good cheer all who do so. Believe what you give, whether great or small or little, you do God's work. He knows, he watches, and he loves.

Remember, he who gives of his talents gives as much as the fairest angel of the land.

130

Desmond's Story

I remember a dark and stormy night long ago in a little fishing village where I once lived. I was but a lad of seventeen. I thought I was grown up and knew all about life. Nobody could tell me what was what. I knew the lot.

I was to be a fisherman, just like my dad and his dad before that. For generations, we had fished along this Cornish coast. It was not a trouble to me to think that. I knew no other life. It was all that I had hoped for.

Money was tight, but we went without nothing. Mother would say each day, 'Count your blessings, my boy, and you will see how rich you really are.' Life was good and the fish plenty. I could see no black clouds on the horizon.

I tell you my story with love and longing in my heart. Love for my life. Longing, for it has been taken away from me.

Despair not, my dear reader. I come just to say a gentle reminder for you to count your blessings this day and see just how rich you are.

131

I shall tell my story. It may be glum and shallow. It may seem a daring plan but tell it I must.

There once was a young lady, very bonny in looks, that cared for her family. Her father worked away, and her mother was always ill and could do very little. So, she cooked, cleaned and washed for them. Her days were never her own. There seemed little joy in her life, but this was how it was meant to be.

Her days melted one into another. Nights were never long enough. She could see no end to this drudgery. She caught a chill and died. She was no more.

Stepping over to the other side was so smooth and effortless that it took time for her to comprehend what had happened.

Gone were the demands on her. Gone the daily grind of looking after others. She was free and yet not free of her obligation to others.

Bliss is sometimes a fanciful cliché that rolls off the tongue of the initiated. The contentment of a job well done can be the panacea of the oppressed.

The giving of oneself may seem, to others, a valiant drudgery to validate their existence, but look ye no further when it comes to being heroic.

Those that seek their reward in heaven will and must be disappointed, for the Lord sees and knows what is in your heart and not in your head.

132

Miriam's Story

I pick up this pen today to tell you all of your tomorrows. A bold and daring statement, you may say, but I say, 'Not.'

Tomorrow is where your dreams lay. Tomorrow is that dreaded place you do not wish to be. Tomorrow is an adventure. Tomorrow is whatever you want it to be, for you have the power to define all your tomorrows.

Do not leave it to chance. Do not presume that you have no control over your future. You are foolish if you think so.

For do you not realise your power? Do you not see that you create your own tomorrows?

Fate does step in and intervene. Fate does create the alternative to your plans, but fate too can be your friend.

Go. Create your tomorrows today. What you sow today, you will reap tomorrow. It's that easy.

Trust in your choices. Trust in the decisions you make today. Learn from them too. Wrong choices maketh wise men.

Wise choices, be they lucky or be them heart centred, are of your choosing.

So, stop, consider, and then act. But always be vigilant, for in doing so, you create your golden tomorrows.

133

Jacob's Story

The tale I am about to tell you is true. It was a hard lesson that I was to learn, so heed my warning.

An obsession has a power of its own. An obsession blinds you to all others. It destroys the soul.

An obsession can take you unawares. It has an energy all of its own.

An obsession makes you oblivious to all others. It can harm many, and it will harm you.

Have we no control over an obsession? Is it an evil force that pervades our soul so severely that we lose control?

What forces of darkness do we succumb to when obsession enters our psyche? Have we lost control to a higher force? Do we choose to fight it or surrender to it?

The pleasures of surrender are many. The weak surrender. And the brave? Well, how brave are you? What pain are you willing to endure? What length of time will it take to bring you back to reality?

134

Samuel's Story

When is a man, not a man? When he is alien to his brother.

When is a man not a man? When he goes against God's law.

When is a man not a man? When greed and petulance are his masters.

When is a man not a man? When he sees himself as equal to all.

When is a woman not a woman? When she decries her femininity.

When is a woman not a woman? When greed and petulance are her masters.

When is a woman not a woman? When she becomes Mother Earth.

When all men seek the common good, when love rules their hearts, then can we all touch the stars? Then can we become masters of our destiny?

135

Thomas's Story

A boat sailing on the water, what vision does that conjure up for you? A sailboat, a paper toy boat, a sleek yacht, a working tugboat. Many concepts, many ideas.

Play with that thought. Many concepts, but basically, all the same. All floating. All going somewhere. All with a purpose.

People can be like that. All the same, yet all different.

Do we see paper boats as cheap and flimsy? Do we see glamorous sleek gliding yachts as expensive, out of our reach? Dirty well-worn tugboats, look but do not touch?

We judge on looks. We take what we see with our eyes, it being 'what it is', no other, and we miss the point. We are blind to their function. We miss their input to society.

We are all sailing in the same direction. When we get there is not for us to judge.

Does clothing maketh the man? I think not, and deep down, you, too, know it.

So, stop and not prejudge. Consider who clothes the lilies in the field and the flowers in the hedgerow. They all smell as sweet. They all colour our world.

136

Samuel's Story

It is I, Samuel, he who is now in spirit but has longed to make contact to all on the Earth plane. I have been waiting a long time to share my philosophy. I grant you this message in the hope that whoever reads it will learn gratitude for all blessings that we receive from Source.

Today may seem mundane. This day may seem just like any other day. Quite ordinary. Yet this day that has just begun is the best day of your life.

'And why', you may ask, 'should this be so?' For nothing is planned. You can see nothing exciting – just a plain ordinary day with only the normal routine of everyday living.

But wait awhile. I stop you in your tracks to remind you who giveth this day to you.

Does it not seem reasonable that you were to survive the night? It was to be expected, and yet millions have not. Their time has come to leave this Earth.

Quite a daunting concept. Makes you think, does it not? We all take for granted that we still see tomorrow (for it has been, so it will always be).

Ah, my dear friends, may I remind you that tomorrow is just the hope of the majority, and that gratitude is in the minority.

137

Roger's Story

I come this day to bring to you a dear fellow with the given name of Roger. He is of an ancient age. His longing to share is much. I leave you in his hands.

The text I chose today is on CONSTANCY. Constancy in all its trials and in all its connotations.

Constancy is a difficult concept for those who flit through life drifting here and there, never laying down roots and never believing that 'this is all there is in life'.

Constancy is dedication. It knows that, at last, one has found a purpose, a distant goal yet to be achieved.

Constancy deserves recognition. Constancy in all things may become the habit that we all live by.

Constancy can be good or can be bad. Is it just another word for habit? But constancy, whether good or bad, is YOU. Your way. Your belief system.

Change is difficult. Change is seeing beyond your usual concept of 'what is'.

So, be constant in your approach to change. Change for change's sake is not good. It leads to confusion. But by being constant in your approach to a better life, you are open to guidance and greater knowledge.

138

Rachel's Story

Have you ever wondered why, at this precise moment in time, you are where you are? Sitting on a train reading this book, tucked up in bed, or even lying on the beach in the sun?

What has brought you to this moment in time? Choices?

Maybe. Maybe not in the bigger scheme of things we miss, for life trundles by without us ever realising that a pattern is being formed. We miss the synchronicity of it all.

Retract your steps just for a moment. Look and see what it was that put you into this situation.

Is a bigger picture being formed? The realisation that an unseen guiding hand has been steering you to this moment?

How does it feel? Good, bad, comforting or with resentment and anger, this is where you do not want to be?

See through the mist of your conditioning. Try seeing the bigger picture and smile when you do so. As soon as you do, you will agree that this is the best place to be.

139

Barbara's Story

Barbara comes forth, a little lady but big in heart. A granny to many and an angel to all.

I once had a cat. He was big and black with green eyes. I always thought of him as wise, with an air of knowing about him.

On rare occasions, he would join my company and allow me to pet and stroke him, but he knew when I needed a friend.

He knew when my world was broken and lost. He knew when he was needed. He knew he could help. He watched, he waited, and he was always there before I knew that I needed help.

I bless his memory. I still miss him. He did not speak, but he knew all that was needed of him.

They say that animals are 'dumb'. They speak a different language that we fail to understand. But the failure is in us.

They know the language of LOVE. They know that words are not important. 'Actions speak louder than words', 'by your actions ye are known'.

Be that 'dumb' animal. Watch and wait, for the gift of LOVE is all that is needed.

140

Jonathan's Story

Jonathan greets you with this message. He knows from experience the wasted time that he spent when opportunity was there and never acted upon.

I hold up my hand this day and say STOP. Stop and consider where your life is going.

I see you frown. I see you hesitate. I guess this question has never entered your head before. Let's consider this question.

Ponder awhile. Let your imagination take control. Is it so far-fetched what you are now imagining? Do the realms of fantasy overtake you? To dream the impossible dream!

What if you could make this your reality? Have you never had a dream come true?

So, the next question is, what are you waiting for? Begin your dream. Plan your next step. Plan each and every step until you get there.

I write in haste, for time is short. Your time is not to be wasted.

'Impossible', I hear you shout.

The only person, the only handicap to fulfilling that dream, is YOU.

Why dream? Make it happen. You have the power to do so.

Go with my blessings. Go begin your climb. Never look back on your 'might have beens'. Only see that, through your own guts and determination, victory is yours.

Cannot be bothered? Then your life is over – the real life you were meant to live.

141

Clara's Story

I once owned a pony called Dobbin. He was the love of my life. Days we would spend together. He was my best friend.

As in all things, nature develops. Nature grows and moves us on.

There came a sad time when I had to move on to leave him behind as I grew too big to ride him.

We said our goodbyes, knowing we would never see each other again – he to a new owner, me to the making of a new friend. I shall never forget him, for such love stays with us.

Friendships in all walks of life can be like that. Love that once was shared, 'ships that pass in the night' you may say, for no other reason they leave us, ponder awhile on this.

Do they come and touch our lives for a reason? Have lessons to be learned in the knowing of them, and why the pain in their leaving?

Is life teaching us a lesson? Do we out-grow their friendship? Does their energy cease to be compatible with ours?

Trouble yourself not, for I believe that friends are sent for a particular reason, for the playing out of that time together is necessary for development – theirs and yours.

So, bless all your long-forgotten friendships and the people who have passed us by. Bless them for the time that they chose to spend with you. Thank them for the memories. Treasure them, for I know they treasure memories of you.

142

David's Story

I bring you a great man of worthy stature. He lived long on the Earth plane. He was a learned gentleman, a great statesman in his county, a wise and gentle soul who you will love. I give you David.

I lay before you this thought, this gesture of peace and solidarity that all mankind can comprehend. It does not take a great education or a great accomplishment of knowledge to know that peace can prevail on the Earth plane.

We, in the realms of spirit, see and watch with sadness at the distress that you have created. I place before you all this resolve, this token, this thought, these choices that if made with the belief that someday very soon the 'little man' in the street, yes YOU, will topple these mighty governments with their belief system that all wars must end. The taking up of arms is not the answer.

When will the killing stop? When all our young men have died and are no more? What will it take for you to realise this?

I do not advocate a rebellion. I do not see the laying down of arms. The urge to fight is in us all, yet I ask you to look deep within your hearts at the consequences of your actions.

You have heard this all before. You have sat through many a political speech on such a topic. I see tolerance being the main concept of the majority, those people who think that they have no power to improve the situation. But here comes the big clincher – YOU DO.

All ye 'little people', I shout out loud to you. You

do have the power to change the world.

Club together. Rise and become the next political force.

Too big an issue? Too scary? Which then do you prefer? Life as it is now (pause and think) or the life you dream of?

Remember what a colony of ants can achieve. Those tiny creatures, weak on their own, but mighty when they move en masse.

143

Caroline's Story

I bring to you this day a solemn little lady whose troubles I am sure you can help her with. Caroline is her name. A blessed and worried soul whose concern is with you all this day.

It was on a dark and rather drizzly grey day when the entire world seemed to have gone to ground. Doors and windows were all closed to the elements. Nobody was going to risk going out on a day like this day.

Hiding from the weather or hiding from themselves begs the question.

Doom and gloom all around us makes us shrink from the possibility of there being another way.

Do we have to wait for others to bring sunshine into our lives? Is the expectation of others our demise?

You be that ray of sunshine that brightens up the sky of others, even though perhaps someone else 'rains on your parade'.

For if you do, you will see that one by one, the clouds on your own horizon will disappear, and the sun in your sky will once again appear.

144

Matthew's Story

It is said of many that all who seek the 'common good' shall 'know the kingdom of heaven', or simply 'by your actions ye are known'.

The story I now reiterate may clarify this for you.

As we travel along our rocky road of existence, meeting here and there, crossing our path from one existence to another, memories of your time spent with other souls leave their mark.

You may not be aware of this. The memory of some long-forgotten incident has passed you by, but others remember, whether good or bad, pleasant or uncomfortable.

The imprint we make on other people is of far greater consequence than you can imagine.

Memories play false tricks on our minds. What is a good and happy memory to someone is a painful embarrassment to others.

My point I bring to you is this. My impression I wish to make to you is simply being aware of your manner, your thoughts, and your actions. Why, even the tone of your voice lingers with another.

We all like 'happy memories' of long-forgotten people and situations, but occasionally, the other sort rears its ugly head, returning to haunt us, leaving a bad taste and a dreadful regret that we failed to be our best.

What has gone has gone. Leave it with no regrets. Leave with the knowledge of your future, of a determination to be ever watchful, to be ever mindful of just how important we are in the scheme of things.

Do not be deceived that 'time heals all'. Time and regret will haunt you until you forgive yourself.

145

Clare's Story

I come today out of a sense of duty. A sense that I am one of the lucky ones among you. I may be dead and in spirit, but I feel as if I still share all your problems, all your fears, as well as your achievements. I am here to explain to all who would read my words – a little story to illustrate where I'm at and why I am here.

I begin by blessing you all this day. I bless each and every one be ye old or young, be ye infirmed or in health. By reading my message, I long to share the joy I am feeling at making contact with you.

You all take for granted friends, colleagues, next-door neighbours, family, shop assistants (I could go on), everyday life, and everyday chores. Everyday 'doings' are what make and enrich our lives.

Boring to some, mundane and monotonous to the majority, but to the minority of people, contact is their basic food for life.

Imagine, can you? Imagine yourself on a desert island. No one and nothing for miles as far as the eye can see. Not even a bird's call or the buzzing of a bee. Silence. Complete and utter silence.

Peace or hell? Perfection or torment? We were never meant to be alone. Even the so-called loner is never on his own, for you recognise him as a loner.

Be aware of others. Be aware of just how many people fill our lives. Ye are blessed. Ye are fulfilling your lives as they were meant to be lived.

Pity the rich man in his castle and the fortress he has built to keep others out. Be relieved that your life is ordinary. You can reach out and touch and be touched by your fellow man, and no barriers divide you.

146

Benjamin's Story

I remind you that this day, this blessed day, has been given by the almighty grace that is God your Father. He seeks not to judge you. His benevolence is much, a grace that is yours by right. He comes not to judge you but to coax you into a bigger belief in the small-mindedness that prevails in your thoughts.

You are to look beyond that thought pattern that is you at this very minute. He hastens you into an awareness of the light. The urge is strong. It is essential, for time is not on your side. Time is now, not tomorrow. This precise moment is all the time you have. Do not delay. It would be fatal to do so, for the Lord your God gives only to those who seek him out.

'A harsh judgement', I hear you say, but all know this. All are aware. There is not one soul living who does not know, deep down in his psyche, that truth and justice must prevail. They fool themselves if they believe any other.

A short sharp shock I bring to you who refuse to listen to that small voice that only seeks to remind you of this fact.

Believe it when it halts you. Believe when panic arises. Believe it when doubt creeps in.

Go now. Think about what I have said. Go and remember the pact you made aeons ago.

Do you forget? I think not. No excuses. No blaming of others, for no such circumstances have ever been beyond your control.

147

Mary's Story

Mary comes. Mary is here, the blessed mother of our Lord Jesus Christ. I come to share with you and all who will read your book. You seek to serve. You know the importance of the work that is done here. I speak to all who would listen and read my words. Be blessed and know it is a true record of my words.

I smile on you all this day, this glorious day that is just beginning. A new life begins this day. What will this day bring? What joys, what plans have you for this day?

The unseen may rear its head but fear not, for many a problem is sent to you for a purpose.

Challenges are brought to you for your growth and to give you strength. They may come at the most inopportune moment, but problems never come at a good moment.

How to handle a problem that springs to our minds. Do we panic? Do we cry 'help' to that unseen force that we hope is there listening to us? If you believe, then it is so.

To the doubters amongst you, I smile and say, 'Why?' For do you not realise all that has gone on before you and all the unseen forces that wait on you? There were times when help came through when not even asked for, so why would we desert you now?

We in spirit watch and wait. We hold you in our hands. We never let another be harmed if it is not in God's plan, so why would we ignore the cries of our children? We are here. We only seek to serve. We are here to show you love and compassion for all true hearts who seek the common good.

It is easy. Believe, and it will be so.

I leave you now with this loving thought. By your actions, ye are known, and by your hearts, ye are known to us.

148

Donald's Story

Animals. Let's talk animals. Are you a lover of animals, God's little creatures, all furry, all feathery, some friendly and some wild and unattainable?

By love, I mean respect. Respect for all of God's creatures. The concept that they have a right to consideration, to dignity, to be guarded when endangered, and to be cared for when captured.

Our furry friends, the cute and cuddly ones, set us no problems. Our feathered variety also.

But what of the wild, untamed ones? Do we see them as a threat, a liability and an expense the world cannot afford? Does the interference of conservationists with their begging bowls annoy you?

Why should we be bothered with endangered species? What use are they anyway?

Pause awhile. Set yourself apart from your usual concept, and see with different eyes that once these magnificent creatures go, they can never be replaced.

Again, you shrug with bewilderment, 'Don't care, not important'.

But please consider this. Judgement in all things sets us apart from the rest of the herd. The allowing to 'live and let live', please make that your motto. In doing so, you are blessed with tolerance to all of God's creatures.

149

MANTRA

God is love, God is love, God is love.
God is great, God is great, God is great.
God is just, God is just, God is just.

God is love, God is love, God is love.
God is here, God is here, God is here.
God is you, God is you, God is you.
You are God, you are God, you are God.

You are God's love, God's love is in you.
You are peace, peace is you.
You are eternal, God is eternal.
God is love, you are God's love.

God is love, God is love, God is love.
God is great, God is great, God is great.
God is just, God is just, God is just.

God is love, God is love, God is love.
God is here, God is here, God is here.
God is you, God is you, God is you.
You are God, you are God, you are God.

You are God's love, God's love is in you.
You are peace, peace is you.
You are eternal, God is eternal.
God is love, you are God's love.

Clare's Story

Make it quick. Make it sharp. Make your mark.

Dear one, be not all haste this day. Commitments are many. That elusive thing called time that runs ahead of you as you battle to catch up.

Look outside your window. What do you see? What images are there before your eyes?

Do the leaves on the tree grow any faster? Do the flowers shed their leaves any faster? No, there is a time. There is a season for such things.

'Making time' is a saying that is often talked about by all who neglect their duty. But time is on your side when you first open your eyes to greet the day.

How you use your time depends on the appreciation of that God-given commodity.

Use it well. Use it to your advantage, for time is precious. Do not fail it, for perhaps this time is all you have.

151

Sheila's Story

Blessed are the meek, for they shall inherit the Earth.'

A wise and noble saying. A quotation you all know. But let's break it down. Let's analyse it, for my understanding may contradict yours.

Who seeks to bless the meek and the disadvantaged? Who gives us false hope of a better life?

Those of you, who have a great belief in your gods, are perhaps the blessed ones.

What of those who disbelieve? Are they doomed forever more from this wonderful fantasy world?

I see I shock you. You expected a great explanation from all that is beautiful. I seek not to be impertinent. I seek not to be abrasive. I only plead for your understanding of those less fortunate who have no learning of such matters.

Pray for them. Pray that they may once find the peace and hope that has been given to you.

For you are indeed blessed. The chosen one. You have no excuse of being saved from this turmoil of your immediate existence.

152

Martha's Story

When the day begins, and the people in our life seem miles away from your existence, do not despair. The knowledge that can never be shared is only the lack of courage that is born out of ignorance. We do not want to look foolish in the eyes of others, but that is our pre-judgement and not how it can be.

The preconception that we expect, that we feel in the judgement of others, is our downfall.

Were other inventors, other people of notoriety, ever taken on this journey of disbelief? Without their courage, electricity would never have been invented. The world would never have been explored.

Your achievements may not rate as highly as theirs, but your achievements are no less worthy.

Stand back and consider where you were, say, ten years ago. Do you not see what I mean? I see your smile. You all see. You all know just how far you have progressed in your job, in your learning, or the bringing up of your children.

The awareness that progress brings cannot be denied. As you grow, so you change. Others see this. It takes time for you to appreciate that change in yourself.

Do not despair when the people who may benefit from it cannot share knowledge that is known to you. Have patience with those who refuse to listen. You know the truth. Let them seek their own, for the belief that is iterated from one to another only seeks to shorten their learning.

So, despair not. Wait. Just wait until they seek

your wisdom. You will be surprised how far you have come, for wisdom comes with age, not 'on a wing and prayer.

153

William's Story

William is here. I bring to you a little lad who was once a paper boy in his past life. An accident took his life. He went before he could make his mark in the world. Grant him this opportunity to do so.

A word to the grown-ups. Do I have your attention? I come today to say to all a gentle reminder (for I know of the anger this may cause) to put aside your memories of your childhood.

The sins of the father are not always passed down to your offspring. Judgement, the expectation that you have produced the next Einstein, becomes a battle of wits. Step aside now and again. Step back and let us breathe our own air.

You think that sometimes maybe we lack your judgement, your tolerance and understanding of a given situation, but remember, dear elders, you were once young and carefree. We never needed to look beyond the next hour.

Tolerance comes with age and patience, likewise.

We try to conform, and we do aim to please, but the concept that we lack is knowing who to please – you or our higher selves.

154

Desmond's Story

I am now an old man. I have lived or existed on the Earth plane for many lifetimes. This is my resting time, but to share would be my greatest joy.

May the noise that you hear, when the calling of the birds bid you arise from your slumbers, only seek to acknowledge their existence.

Their role in life is not your call to a new day. It is your awakening to remind that others, lesser known, are there about you.

Many birds and many different calls. Some loud and constant, some sweet and melodious, all welcomed to your hearing.

Is it just a noise or a reawakening to a reminder of their existence?

We all take for granted that they are there, like humans, the voices in the street as they pass you by.

Voices, noise, speech, and bird calls are all similar, all drawing your attention to their existence and needing to be recognised.

Is it a pain or a joy to hear their existence? A bother or a comfort? You decide.

But remember, you, too, have a voice. What noise do you make? What reception is greeted by your calling?

155

Jane's Story

I once had a necklace. A beautiful blue stoned necklace. I only wore it on special occasions. I was so afraid of losing it. Many admired it. It made me feel special. I held this necklace in such high esteem that nothing else I owned matched its importance.

When I wore this necklace, I changed from the mundane me into a beautiful creature that attracted all around me. Or so it seemed.

Then one day, taking my necklace out of its box, it broke. The clasp broke. Horror upon horror, panic like I never knew before, filled me. What was I to do?

I could never be that ravishing beauty and never be that other person. No one would see me as I wanted to be.

It was too late to get it mended that day. The event was about to begin. Confidence had left me. Confidence was no more.

I think you can guess how my story will end.

Stupidly I had relied on one inanimate object, a crutch that I thought I needed to become the real me.

'Foolish is, as foolish does.'

Stop, dear one. Think on this thought. Let my story be your lesson on the dependence we put on any object, whether male or female, and now resist.

You have no need for ornamental adornments. No pretence. The beauty that is you will shine through. The beauty is there for all to see.

156

Arthur's Story

I give to you this day a fable, a story of much magic and notoriety, that many must think hard on its message. It is short and to the point. Maybe the point is not to your liking but a truth nonetheless.

Stop. This day I challenge you to stop and be counted upon to declare your intent to all your brothers and sisters that come your way.

Have you patience? Have you concern for their welfare?

Does it bother you that perhaps their world is not as clear or bright as yours?

Are you aware that perhaps that chance meeting was not the coincidence that you first thought? What difference will you make to your acquaintance? What words of advice, comfort, or sharing of laughter will occur?

The giving of just one of your words could and will make the difference between their joy and dismay. Believe it to be so, for change is that enigma that binds us together.

Do not run and hide from that fellow who only seeks to put you down or who drains you of all your energy and vitality. Challenge him to your light.

Set yourself a test. See if your light can shine in his darkness. Light up just one corner of his existence and then stand back and watch.

157

Luke's Story

All our Tomorrows' is the title of this book, dear reader. You have come so far in your journey. I know you enjoy the book you have meticulously read because you have come so far.

What of your tomorrows, your dreams, your hopes and your longings? That wish that you hold onto so tightly, your secret desire that none know of, for fear or ridicule?

They say that tomorrow never comes, so do we dream idly, wasting our time? You and I both know that it is not so.

Dreams do come true. I expect some of you have experienced it so. But dreams beget dreams and so on.

I wish all your 'tomorrows' come true. I wish that your star shines for you.

We have never met, well, not in this lifetime, but maybe, just maybe, my wish for you comes true. Will you then believe that you do not have to wait? For 'tomorrow' is now.

158

Today was like any other day, or so he thought. He had woken much earlier than normal.

'Why', he wondered, 'no need to be awake this early. It's not time for work yet.'

'I shall read', he thought, 'catch up with my reading. Yes, that is a good idea.'

Settling himself down to read, where was his place in the book?

His marker was lost. Oh dear, where was he in the scheme of things? Was he to start at the beginning or guess and continue halfway through the book?

Is life like that for you? Are you lost in the book of life? Where are you in the scheme of things? Could you go back to the beginning and start all over again? Would you if you could?

You don't have to. The place where you are at is where you should be. Right here, right now at this moment, is where all your past is accumulated.

The theory that 'if I could only go back. If only I knew then what I know now' does not apply, for it is in not knowing that the lessons have been learned.

So where are you in the scheme of things? In a place where you choose to be? If not, change it.

159

Barbara's Story

When we are young, time for us moves so slowly. Birthdays never come quickly enough, and Christmas seemed even longer. We knew that time was on our side because we were young. Our whole lives, all those years lay there waiting for us to use up.

We would idly dream our days away, waiting for that time when we were grown up and leading our own lives. No more authority. We could please ourselves what we did, where we could go, and even where we chose to live. We thought that being grown up meant freedom.

But, as in all things, we soon learned that growing up meant responsibility. When this dawns on us, it is too late. We were already a grown-up, dreaming of being a child again.

Confusion or contradiction, never being satisfied?

What would it take for you to be satisfied with your life at this present moment? Or have all your needs been met?

You are indeed blessed if that is the case. You can count yourself lucky for all your hard work has come to fruition.

And all the rest of you? Well, keep trying. Keep working at it. It will come, the satisfaction of a job well done. The giving of your best is all that is expected of you.

160

The day begins as many other days have begun – cold and wet. She looked out of the window and sighed. Perhaps today, the sun will shine. Perhaps not.

It was a belief system of hers to always 'look on the bright side'. She did try. But at times, it was so difficult, what with children and her complaining husband. Where was she? Where was she in all of this?

The books she had read talked about being 'positive and of being in the now'. How she did try. Sometimes it was easy, especially when the sun shone and it was payday. But today, where had that warm cosy glow gone? Perhaps it will return tomorrow.

The day wore on. She busied herself with all the mundane jobs that called for her attention. Having finished everything she had planned for that day, she made herself a cup of tea.

'Just five minutes', she said, 'it's time for a break.' She slowly sipped her tea, gazing into the warm, steaming liquid. There floating on the surface was a little dark speck of something. Retrieving it, she placed it on the back of her hand. It grew until it covered the back of her hand.

Quite alarmed at this, she went to destroy it. It became opaque. She could see through her own hand, see bone and muscle, and see blood pumping through the veins.

Fascinated by what she was viewing, time slipped, and her reality was no more. She saw herself in a different light, the mechanics of her workings.

It seemed odd. She had never perceived herself

as anything other than what she viewed in the mirror. Fascinated at all of this, her mind slipped again to focus on another dawning in her mind.

She was much more than surface. She, in all her glory, was a walking, breathing miracle. She was special!

No more a drudge. No more a servant of others. How could she have been so blind as not to see that the Creator had made her more than surface?

She smiled at this realisation. She was special and worthy of respect and a position in society.

Her day began to glow. This is a new start. Now my world begins, and to this day, I bring a new meaning into my life. I am reborn.

The scene faded, and the skin grew back. How could I have ever doubted that the Son, my Son, would shine for me?

161

Good morning world. A very good morning to you, indeed. All is happy, all is joy, all is smiles, and all is goodwill to men.

'Dream on', I hear you shout, 'dream another dream this day'.

The bank manager has been on the phone, the kids are playing up, noisy neighbours and barking dogs. I could go on with my list. (This is where I let your own misery enter this page.)

Problems. We are always surrounded by them. Some are little and not worth mentioning, and some are so huge that they constantly pervade our thoughts, never letting us be.

How to handle a problem is worth considering. Many choices and many advisers. A neighbour down the road, a qualified consultant, or a large bottle of gin, perhaps? Or do we make ourselves so ill that we go too far?

(You may detect a more serious note, a more alarming connotation, but I need to be serious to point out the danger you place yourself in.)

We all know and care for our fellow man, be it a stranger in the street or our dear and devoted friends. Do we seek their reassurance on how to handle our problems, or are we too embarrassed to confess them?

They say that a 'problem shared is a problem halved'. Do you believe that? Do you believe that only sharing your problem with another solves that problem? If that is so, then all is easy. All it takes is to speak out loud, but to whom?

Be careful whom you choose, for trust must play a big part in this scenario. But I know of a great and noble person. I know him and so do you, can you guess?

I play a game. It is he who loves you, he who is your Father, and he who made you. Why it is none other than your friendly almighty God who looks down and sees you suffer so.

Go to him. Talk to him. He has all the solutions, you only have to ask, and it is so.

162

The story I now begin to share is perhaps not of your liking but a true story you will never hear.

It all began one dark and stormy night as she sat alone, waiting for her beloved to return.

He was late. This was not unusual, as was his habit of keeping her waiting. How many times had this happened? She began counting. There was this occasion, that occasion, oh so many she lost count. But wait she did. It was her habit to do so.

But this night felt different. She tried to ignore the panic that was arising in her heart. Fear began to invade her. Why tonight? Why now? What is so special about this time? Her imagination grew wilder.

My tale I leave there. You must judge. Can you not see the situation in your mind's eye? Have you ever been in that situation? Loss of another and the dependability we place on others. It is human to do so, for 'no man is an island', and yet love clouds the issue. Love leaves us vulnerable, but we can become strong again and gain strength in love.

(He did return, and all was well in the end.)

I only tell my story to make all aware of the vulnerability that is placed in us humans. It is not a problem, I am sure. You can see for yourself that we grow strength purely from that one thought.

So where do we go when fear and vulnerability invade our persona? Who or where is that place that we cling to, cry to?

We cry to heaven. We cling to His strength. Make no mistake. He is there. He is there waiting for your call. He is your strength. He is your 'dependable rock', and He will never keep you waiting.

163

Sing a song for me. Sing it loud, sing it long and sing it sweet. For indeed is not your voice the sweetest of all?

Shame if you think not. For this is how we were meant to be, how we were meant to live.

'Begone dull care, begone from me.'

I echo these words. These old-fashioned words, but if one puts them into practice, why how the soul is lifted.

You try for yourself. Go and see if I am right. What have you to lose? You have all to gain.

164

It came upon me while walking one day in the woods, the thought that what we see is not what we believe in.

Why is man so blind to the obvious? Why does man only seek to judge and prejudge others before he knows both sides of the coin?

It shames me. It bothers me to think about how we shut ourselves away from others because we do not understand their differences.

The sadness grew on me. The weight became so insurmountable that I could not breathe. What was I doing to myself? What was I becoming? What was I losing?

I was losing the will to breathe naturally. The burden I was carrying was leaving me short of breath. The very life of me was being taken away under this burden. What was I doing taking all the troubles of the world onto my shoulders? And it was killing me.

I dropped to the ground to rest, to try to catch my breath, the breath that I needed to carry me on.

Then it dawned on me. The realisation hit me, is this what we are doing to each other? Is this what we are doing to our beautiful world? Squeezing the lifeblood out of her? Why, we deserve to die. We deserve to lose this precious gift if we refuse to cooperate to live in harmony.

For lying there on the ground beneath the trees, I understood. I understood that if nature in all her rawness can live in harmony, so should we. Enlightened being that we profess to be (one step above the animals) but are we, are we there yet?

165

In the beginning it was said, 'He that is of lowly birth, yet shall he rise to a great height.'

Is that a statement for you to latch onto? Is that a belief of yours, a possibility that each of us can succeed, or just a pipe dream of some distant philosophy?

She thought about the possibility of succeeding, to be up there amongst the hierarchy. A dream, just a dream. And yet, perhaps no. She was mortal, but other mere mortals had achieved stardom. Fame and glory were theirs, so why not? Maybe, just maybe.

She smiled at her thoughts. Her disbelief that she was special, and yet the flicker of 'what if' would not go away. Her reasoning continued. Her mind skipped along the pathways of possibilities. Her daydreaming knew no bounds.

She saw herself surrounded by glory. Just a little bit of sunshine or a glow of recognition was all she wanted or even needed. She smiled to herself. Such a fantasy. Such a rich reward. She had to pinch herself.

How she did laugh. What a fool am I. Why little old me would run a mile with the thought that life could be any different than the one she was already living.

To daydream is our right. To feel special is our right. For what are we but children of no lesser God than him who sits on a throne or captains of industry?

We are who we are. We each play a special role in the mechanics of life.

A teacher is as vital as a doctor is as vital as a road sweeper. We are here for a purpose, and your role in life is as blessed as any other.

To dream, to be a dreamer, is a blessed and noble trait. So do not laugh at your dreams. Do not see them as impossible, for man in his wisdom knows all is possible. If only we see our dreams as an escapement, but much more than that, more than a 'what if'.

What are the chances at our birth of being in the right place at the right time? Only not as a lottery but as the chosen place we choose to be.

166

William's story

There once was a big and hairy dog that bullied all the other dogs in town. The owner did not seem to care about his welfare. This dog would roam the streets, terrifying any other animal that strayed into his path. Children and parents, too, gave him a wide berth when they saw him approach. He thought himself king of the road. King in his own little town.

The bullying continued until one day, a stranger came to town in the shape of a cat.

Now, this was no ordinary cat. His name was Marcus, and many a fight he had been in when rivalry had set in as to who was to be 'top dog' in his neighbourhood. Marcus always won. But being an old cat, he had mellowed, letting others pursue notoriety. He preferred the quiet life.

Word got around that there was a stranger in town. Conflict was bound to ensue.

The meeting was to be held on an old rubbish tip far out of town, for this would be a sight you would wish not to see.

The day dawned sunny and bright. Positions had been taken up, and the duel was about to begin.

Suddenly a little boy appeared on the scene (not realising that war was about to be declared) and spotted the two animals squaring themselves up to each other. He raced over to pat the dog and cuddle the cat.

The animals gasped in amazement. Never before had anyone been brave enough to show such affection. He showed no fear. He relished the thought that he could maybe own this dog, for it seemed to need love and attention.

Taken aback by all of this, the two animals stepped back to allow the child the decision of whom to choose.

Suddenly the child began to sing a sweet and melodious song, straight from the heart, straight to your heart.

The animals dropped back, ashamed of what could have happened. What was the point? What had they to prove? If being 'top dog' in your life, in your circle of friends and companions, is all you clamour for, stop and see who it is that pets and loves you. Perhaps the animals, in their wisdom, know a greater truth.

167

As we wander through our lives each day exactly like the last, with the odd exception of a disaster here, or a wonderful event there, we perceive rightly or wrongly that this is how life was meant to be. We expect to leap from one disaster to another. Many dales with just a few peaks. So be it if that is all you expect from your life.

But is that all there is? Are you contented with this existence? Could there be another way? Should there be another way?

'Mustn't grumble' comes the reply when someone asks, 'How are you today?'

I say grumble. I say shout and scream if you need to. Why suffer? Why the heavy shoulders?

Do you not realise that there is help out there? There are people, seen and unseen, who are waiting to be asked. They stand waiting, so you have no excuse and no reason not to declare 'all is well in my life. All is sweetness and harmony.'

Do you doubt me? I see you frown. Go and try for yourself. Go and see if I am not right, for what have you to lose? There is a world out there waiting for you to enjoy. Be at peace, my friend.

Stop and consider why others glow with radiance and energy that you wish was yours. Perhaps they are the ones who know of this secret that I now share with you.

168

I would rather not be here today. I would rather be down there on the Earth plane with you. For you see, I dwell in the realms of spirit.

My time on Earth was bleak, to say the least, but I have learnt well. I have learnt my lesson on the forces of evil, corruption, and what it can bring to the soul.

Beware of complacency. Beware of the belief that once you are dead, nothing remains.

Beware of believing that you know best and that the choices you have made are all that there is. This is not so. Beware of the ego. That false prophet that only seeks to rule you.

Beware, just be aware of the thrill of control, of knowing that power is your adrenaline.

Beware, I cry. Be aware of how easy it is to fool oneself into a false sense of security when others back away from you in fear and intimidation.

I have learnt a great lesson. I now know that foolish is as foolish does. I now know that the power I thought I possessed was ultimate, that that was all there was.

The sense that now possesses me is not one of incrimination, not of a snivelling slob that I so despised in others, but of an understanding that to subject another to degradation is a false god. A blot on the soul of humanity.

I cringe at my past doings. I realise that in the fullness of time, my time of recompense, I will have to serve, to right the wrongs and to ask for forgiveness of the souls that I destroyed.

Forgiveness is hard. Forgiveness is my punishment, and forgiveness for myself is the hardest lesson we mortals have to learn.

169

I give you TRUTH.

A word small to spell but vast in its connotation.

Is telling the truth a problem for you? Do you know the difference between a truth and a lie?

When you know the truth that will hurt another, do you see fit to ignore it or lie to them?

Truth is difficult. Truth sets us aside from the herd. Truth tests us when we least expect it.

Truth will see you through even though others treat you with contempt. To prove a truth when others laugh and jeer, to stand one's ground when outnumbered, why, that is the stuff of an angel.

Would you fight for a truth if others were endangered? Is the word truth just another feeble excuse for what is real and unreal in another's eyes? To live by a truth. But who's truth, yours or the fellow next door?

Is truth another word for the doctrine we have been handed down from one generation to another? Has no one ever questioned the truth of another without considering his own beliefs?

The story goes on endlessly. A debate I am sure will continue long after my name is forgotten. And what is my name? Well, it is Jesus.

170

Janice's Story

When I was young, I had many beaus. Many young men sought my hand in marriage. I guess I was pretty, or maybe Papa was rich – I was never sure which.

Who to choose? Which one? Young and handsome or plain with prospects? Mama took me to one side. Her advice she thought I needed. I listened, but all in vain. I was no wiser in choosing a husband.

Time was slipping by me. Friends warned me that I would soon be an old maid, and no one would choose me.

By the age of twenty-three, panic, I guess you would say, began to close in. I noticed that maybe one or two beaus were not available anymore. They had disappeared to join the army, or so I was told.

Mama was in despair. Papa never made any comment, for I was still his 'little girl'.

Decisions of the heart are important. Decisions of the head are they as important?

I began to realise that my wants for a companion had changed. Good looks seemed less important. Instead, the art of conversation took prior place.

I realised that what society expected of me was to follow the herd of previous young women. We were only bred to be companions of the male kind. The more it was expected, the more I resisted.

I say to all young ladies who read my story, let your head rule and do not be misguided by the heart. You are indeed fortunate to be born in enlightened times. Feel pity for us pretty butterflies whose wings society clipped. Be gentle with the male. Do not make him your toy thing. Look and see who it is that rules your heart. Make sure it is you.

171

Holidays. I see you smile – holidays, memories, sunshine, beaches, adventure. To visit distant shores to seek new experiences is what our heart desires.

Some prefer sea and sand mixed with lots of sunshine. Others prefer education, specialised hobbies, touring or visiting many countries in the space of days. Whatever your choice. Whatever your needs.

Why do we go on holiday? What is the pull of visiting distant shores? What motivates us to pack and travel long distances? What are we seeking? What is it that is missing in our lives to do this?

Is it because we can be 'one up' on the neighbours, stating we are rich and can afford such an exotic place? Or is it because our heart and soul long to learn? Long to experience other cultures, join with other people, and see just where 'so and so' was born?

What drives us there? The belief that this is what we have to do? The longing that it brings and the gratification that we have fulfilled a lifetime's ambition when it's been accomplished?

Is your soul telling you something? Is your psyche not fulfilled? That part of you is still seeking a home? How many lifetimes have you had? The world is indeed very small, or is it very large?

How many homes have you had? Or are you still seeking where your next home will be?

172

'I believe that someone in the great somewhere hears every word, I believe, yes I believe.'

Those words pull at the heartstrings. Those of you that have never heard the song have missed much.

Do you believe, or do you hope that it is true that 'someone' hears all our prayers all our cries of help, of pleading, or gratitude?

Does it seem logical to you to ever consider that perhaps we are being duped, that no one really cares about our little problems? For in the scheme of things, what are our problems in correspondence to world poverty, world famine and the arms race?

Does anyone really care about us 'small fry?' We little grains of sand that populate this world of ours. What rights do we have?

Are we fooling ourselves into the belief that there is some magical magician out there waiting for his orders? Waiting to say abracadabra and only granting them if we have been very good and very patient?

I may sound cynical and play the martyr, but I bet you only believe because life has to be better than the one you are now living. And if that is not the case, then let's hope that someone is out there listening to us, for if not, what are we doing wasting his time?

Are you on your own? I'm not, but then I believe.

173

Sheila's Story

Go into your garden this day. What do you see? What do you hear?

Jobs to be done. Clearing out of garbage. More work and not enough time.

Or do you see what is really there? The odd flower struggles to shine for you, and the overgrown bushes that house many sparrows from the weather.

Do you not see what nature, with your help, is constantly proving to you? That against all odds, she will perform her duty?

What of your hearing? Not the noisy neighbour next door or of someone doing DIY. Listen, really listen. Are there birds in your trees? Is there a rustle amongst your weeds? Why your garden is alive with creatures. You may never see them, but they are there, joining you in your space, in your time.

Perhaps you have no garden. Perhaps you and nature never came together. You miss much if that is so. But no excuse is needed, for much around you is available to share.

Please take time. Please share with nature, for she only seeks to soothe and to show you a beauty that is lacking in your day.

174

Guy's story

It all began one day in spring. The weather was crisp and clear. The sun was low in the sky, and the morning frost began to thaw, leaving the air fresh and clean.

I was but a child then, not knowing much about worldly things, but I did know that all was not well in my little world.

I beg to differ when politicians preach to us. They pontificate about 'global warming'. Is it just the latest topic of conversation? Or is it that they like to be heard voicing their opinion on the centre stage? They spout out these words and may be seen to join with others, but they do nothing about it.

They have no answers. They bluff you if they do. Have they not realised that this thing called 'global warming' was meant to be? It is real, and it was meant to be.

Do you doubt me? Do you think what I say is trite? Disasters only occur when man is thrown out of his usual pattern of thinking. He sees change as a disaster. He worries that change has to be for the worst.

Our world is changing, yes, indeed. She changes, for she has a need too. She is young in age and young in her desires. Is the world a place or a collective conscience of its people? To bring about change, good or bad, we need to see what is in our hearts and not our heads.

175

As the day is ending, let us remember long-forgotten friends, people who were once very important in our lives, people who played a significant part in our daily lives.

What became of them, and why did they disappear from our daily lives?

Was it something that was said? Did a situation arrive that made it intolerable to continue that friendship?

People come, people go, and we do not know why. We are at a loss to explain.

Do our lost companions ever think of us?

Do they, too, wonder why we went our different ways? What was it that changed? Was it them, or was it us?

But change happens, life intervenes, and situations arise beyond our control. If we are wise, we accept this. If we are foolish, then we resent this.

What memories have you of your lost friends – good, bad, happy or sad?

You must decide, for it is in remembering that we see the reflection of ourselves.

176

I had a dream last night. Not a nightmare, not quite, but it made me think and consider this question. Who is it that enters our dreams? Who is it that seeks to tell us stories, picture stories?

Is it some guardian angel, some deep-seated desire that only catches our attention when we are sleeping? Is this an invasion of our privacy, for they are never invited?

We do not go to rest with a request for a story to be relayed to us. It just happens unannounced. Strange that one has never debated this question.

But where do dreams come from? Who is it that tells us our stories? Who decides what subject is to be discussed and in what order?

My understanding of dreams is that they are pictures shown to us instead of words, symbols instead of vocabulary, and 'they' presume that we understand.

We blame a restless night on them or something we ate, anything but the truth that someone or something is trying very hard to warn us, to explain, to see our future, to show us the answer to a nagging question.

How to interpret a dream? Many books have been written on the subject. Do you, like me, find them hard to understand, for they never explain your dreams or your symbols.

So, what next? Where do I seek the answer? Perhaps some of you amongst the readers of this book have the answers. As for me, I wait until my dreams become a reality, that elusive feeling that someone, somewhere, is watching out for me, doing their best on my behalf.

I welcome my dreams. I welcome that soul who

seeks to help me. That magical someone who is watching over me.

But I have one request. Please make them simpler. Please help me to remember them more clearly when I awake. For I would love to be able to say thank you to my unseen friend, my guardian angel.

177

Abigail's Story

I love you,' the little boy said to his sister, 'Do you love me?'

'Sometimes,' came the reply.

'Why only sometimes?' he said, feeling very glum.

'Because I just do,' shouted his sister.

'That's no answer,' he shouted back.

'Well, tough, that's how I am feeling. So go away and leave me alone.'

Feeling very dejected, he moved away, far out of her sight. Little did she know of the anguish she had caused.

Much later, she had need of his company, but where was he? He was not to be found.

She was sorry for her harsh words. She did not really mean them. She was sorry. But was it too late? Had the harm been done? Was she lost to him?

Much later, he appeared to try once more to win over his sister. He was back, and she was pleased.

When all the 'sorries' had been spoken, when all the hugging stopped, what had they both learned that day?

We all need a friend, whether we know it or not. Not just for this day, not only on a good day. It's when we least expect it when we discover we are on our own.

178

Jim's Story

Where are you going this day? Who is it that seeks your company? Are you pleased by the expectation of such a meeting? Will time not hurry on? Will it not be 'there' yet?

Have you far to travel? Is your mode of transport to your liking? And the place where you are to meet, does that win your approval?

The topic of conversation, is that important too, or are you merely passing an idle hour or two away? Business or pleasure?

Company is our greatest pleasure, or so it should be. There are those, I suppose, amongst us who are duty-bound to entertain, but the rewards of having accomplished our trial makes us feel quite smug.

I must warn you, though. I must point out to you to be aware that what seemed like a victory at the time comes back to haunt us at a later date.

Choose carefully whom you spend your time with, and always follow the rules.

179

Abigail's Story

I have a very gifted child who had seen and tolerated much while on the Earth plane. Her story is sad, but a great truth she learned because of it. Look and listen and see with different eyes.

One day while out hunting, my father came across a wildebeest that had been injured, so he was dangerous. (The village was hungry. We had not eaten meat in many a long day.)

The animal eyed my father with fear and trepidation, for he knew his time was to be short-lived. His instinct told him to run, but this poor animal had nowhere to run to. His injuries were too severe.

Father called to him to lie down and be quiet. He sensed the troubled animal and saw the fear in its eyes. He knew he had a choice between using his last arrow to ease the suffering of this poor animal or ignoring it to carry on hunting for food.

What would you do? Use your head, not your heart, in making your decision.

Difficult? I think not.

To be practical is all well and good from the safety of your armchair, but in real life, when all future decisions hang on your next move it can be scary stuff.

Let's hope you never have to make a choice, for if you have to, what would be your decision? Where would your loyalty lie? Who is the more important? Who seeks to gain from your next move?

180

I once owned a large dog. He was scruffy and dirty in his habits, but he was mine. He was as faithful as he was wise. We grew up together, Winston and I. We laughed and played many games together, never tiring of each other's company.

There came a time when I had to travel abroad. My job demanded it of me, so Winston was left behind. The months became years, and it was necessary to continue my work abroad. He was well looked after, and others spoilt him, but now and again, when I saw his likeness, my heart would call out to my faithful companion.

One day I was to return and go home. Would he remember me? Had I changed? The anticipation of our meeting filled me with dread. Perhaps he had forgotten me, and he loved his other new family.

I had no need to fear. I had no need to worry, for as soon as we spied each other, oh my, how it all came flooding back. All those years of parting and all those days of missing were gone. Never again would life keep us apart.

I think we both cried with joy at our greeting. I certainly did, and Winston, well as big as he was, became that loveable puppy I once knew. A warm story with a warm ending.

Is there someone somewhere waiting to greet you, waiting to see your face again? They are never far away, not really. Time plays tricks with us. We only think of time as a handicap, a barrier between then and now.

Greet your friends and your loved ones, and meet them in your heart, for distance is no obstacle when love plays its part.

181

This day my dear brother or sister (whoever is reading this book), look and see what this day has given you. Has it been a good day, blessed with happy memories, or a sad and weary day best forgotten?

Are you glad that this day is about to end, or is time rushing by so quickly that you wish you could turn back the clock?

Days come and days go. Some good and some bad. Take the rough with the smooth, we are told.

Remember a day you had not so long ago when all was well in your world. Take it, smell it, feel it now in your heart. Let the remembrance of it fill you up until it consumes you. Relish that thought. Relish the joy that lives within you. See how you grow, how you shine, my dear one. You are victorious. No one can harm you. You are glorious.

Go back to a time of gloom, illness, or problems, and feel how you remember it. Smell it, taste it, live it and ride on it till it consumes you. Then like a puff of smoke, let it go. See it disappear into the air. Sense that choice you have made. Sense the power that is within you.

All is possible. All is proof that it can and will be done in His name, in your name, for you possess His power too. His glory, His strength is your strength. Believe, and it is so.

182

My name is Jane. I am small in stature but very big in my heart.

I look down and see you all. All I can see is rush and push, hectic and heavy. I know life can be so. I know your days are planned far ahead of your existing time. Is this by choice, or have you designed your life to be so?

Order is important and routine, too. And holidays, important 'time out' as you call it, are essential.

Amongst this bustle of your life, where do you come into it? Is your life surrounded by other priorities? Other people first, and then you?

Modesty is all very well sometimes, but I emphasise sometimes, but not every time, in your decision-making. For if you do, if that is your case, then you will slowly, ever so slowly disappear. You will become invisible enough about yourself.

Do not blame others when they ignore you. Don't seethe and boil under your breath, for you have been the cause of such a tragedy.

Wake up. You too, are important. Shout out loud when things do not go your way. Shout and be heard. Do not let your light go out. Do not become the last sheep that follows the herd.

Be brave just this once. How about you being the leader, just this once?

183

I had a dream that I thought would never become a reality. It was a fluke, really, for it never ceases to amaze me when I think of it.

It began one day whilst I was journeying through Spain. We were in the countryside, way beyond any touristy spot. What caught my eye was the shape of the trees. They had somehow changed shape, and a different colour seemed to shine through them.

My companions thought me mad. They thought I was hallucinating at this high altitude, but I knew differently. I knew what I saw.

As we climbed higher into the mountains, true the air was becoming thinner, but I had a feeling of déjà vu. This I kept to myself for fear of being laughed at.

The voice inside my head could not be denied. As much as I tried to ignore it, the more it repeated its message. 'You are home. This is where you belong. See it. Smell it. You are home.'

Our destination was a place called Adeorbia, high in the mountains, a little village with few inhabitants, but this was to be my home.

The air was blue with sounds of shouting coming from a little house on the edge of the village. Two people were arguing. Not understanding the language, I paid no heed to it.

We parked the car, I guess in what you would call the village square. As we got out, people came to greet us, for strangers are rare in these parts. A tall, rather jolly man with great gusto shook me by the hand, beaming the biggest grin you can imagine.

He called my name Padraig. How did he know

me? For I had never been to this place before and never travelled this far north in my life (well, not in this life).

By now, more people had gathered around me, smiling and calling my name. I could not ignore them, so I politely smiled and laughed back.

A small child pushed himself through the crowd. He stopped in amazement at my feet. Shyly he held out his hand and, in broken English, called out, 'This is my Papa'. Words failed me. This is all too much. This is not real. Why me?

My story concludes with little explanation, for I have none. I tried to explain to my friends, but I was told of the resemblance to this child.

Is this a dream or a nightmare? I wanted to run. It was all too much, but the child continued. He took me by the hand and led me to a baker's shop in the town square. As I opened the door, a smiling lady greeted me with such warmth (I could have been her long-lost son).

She called me Pierre and greeted me with a kiss. Then to my surprise, she showed me a photo hanging on the wall. I cried when I saw it. It was me, taken not long ago, for the fashion had not changed. What do I do now? My world seemed to take on a new meaning.

Frantic, I protested this. It was not me, no way. It was not me, but somehow something deep down was telling me something else.

But what of my other life, the one I had left at the bottom of this mountain? Did I prefer that one to this one? Choices – to stay or go back? I needed time. I needed space. The reality of it all hit me. Dare I not stay? No, not possible and yet could it be?

It was then that I woke up. A dream. It had all been a dream. Beautiful but still only a dream.

But it had been so real. Who were those people that recognised me? How and why had it happened? Does our past life catch up with us in our sleep state, or is it a glimpse of the future? Was it a privilege or a nightmare?

Going home becomes our struggle, our constant battle with who we really are. For you have had many lifetimes, many places and many people know of you. Do not deny this privilege, this glimpse of your heritage, for time is an illusion. Time is taken out of context when we see for ourselves who we are and who seeks to reconnect with us.

So be prepared to be amazed when fortune smiles on you, for you are indeed blessed with a rare knowledge of whom you are and of whom you may become.

184

I have a rather sad story to tell you today. It's a story about a little girl called Charlotte. Though she was loved, though she was pretty, folk could not believe her melancholy nature.

She had all a little girl could desire – toys, beautiful dresses and doting parents, yet little did this child ever smile.

She was a contented child. She chose her own company over that of her family and school friends.

Her world consisted of her favourite teddy, her mama doll and nothing else. Boxes and boxes of toys lay untouched. She had no need of them, just her beloved two companions.

Her parents were troubled. How to appease this child? Just to see her run, laugh and play with other children would be their hearts' delight. With no answer that came to them, they sort expert help.

She was taken to see a kind old gentleman doctor. He tried to reach her but to no avail.

'Leave her,' he said. 'Leave her to her own devices. Nature will take its course.'

As the years rolled on, she became a young lady. (Ah, perhaps this could be the turning point.)

Young men came courting, but she would not greet them, and she chose to remain in her room.

Middle age came, then old age. She was reaching her 'end time'. Her time for leaving was upon her.

A sad and lonely figure called Charlotte breathed her last, for now, she could smile, for she was going home.

185

The ways of the wind are known to only a few,
The ways of the sea, though, are known to many,
The ways of the animals are known by the stars.

So, therefore, dear one, who is it that lights your way?
Who is it that watches over you and seeks to guide you?
Who is it that holds you in his hands?
Who is it that will never leave you, no matter how you struggle?
Who is it that loves you, needs you?
Who is it that waits on you, who will never give up hope on you?
Who is it?
Can you not guess, can you not see, can you not believe, for it is so?

Be true to him, who waits on you,
Be true to him, who loves you,
Be true to him, who watches and waits for your return.

186

Mark's Story

Do not let this old world get you down. Do not believe the 'doom and gloomers'. Do not be conditioned by the media. Refuse to buy a Sunday paper and be gone any news bulletins on your TV. Instead, judge the day by your moods. Look and see if the sun shines. See if your neighbour or friend looks to share the day with you.

I wish not to sound naïve or be the proverbial ostrich, but I know my capabilities.

We all see strife and want in our daily lives. We know others suffer. We do what we can, and it is all we can do.

Prayers are good and decrees and wishes too. By being aware of trouble, big problems that seem much or too big for us to solve, we will leave it to the experts.

But who are the experts? Your local MP or your local environmental officer? The government, perhaps? But I think not.

Go and seek a higher authority. Go and leave the problems at their feet. It's that simple.

But be aware of your input, for you are vital to the equations. Your support is needed. You have no idea of the importance of your interference at such a time.

Money is important too. The little you have is all that you have. But by simply adding to all the rest, is how projects as big as a 'dam' can be achieved.

Remember, though, he that believes in the part

he is playing is building up for himself riches in heaven.

187

I call on you today to look around and see with different eyes how your life is progressing.

'Just ordinary. I am just ordinary. No one special, just ordinary.'

Was there ever a time when, oh, let's say, you thought, 'If only I had so and so, how my life would change?' We go on dreaming for that day to arrive.

Is that the only spurt of energy that keeps you going? Is that the only reason to get us up in the morning?

Money is good, and 'if only' becomes our trademark.

Travelling is wonderful. To reach those distant shores could be a dream come true, and yet distant shores could be in the next town. Distant shores become the cliché that we dream and live by.

You who long to experiment, to chance the elements, and to stretch yourselves beyond the mundane are the icons of the oppressed, the moaners and the doubters. We all have the capability to take life by the throat and say, 'Here world, here I am, bring it on down.'

Consider this, why do you not see beyond your noses? Why in all aspects of your life must it be 'doom and gloom?'

Do you not know how rich your life can become just by a mere walk through your local woods? Shake off this lethargy of gloom. Ordinary is boring. Ordinary is not what you are. Believe me? How I wish you could see with my eyes the wonder that you are.

Grab me by the hand and walk with me. I will see that no danger befalls you. Life is an adventure.

Let's explore it together. And who am I that challenges you? Why, none other than your guardian Angel.

188

The story I have for you may seem a little sad, but it is a true and noble saying that 'all who pass this way leave their footprints behind'.

When we make an impression on people, we leave behind our energy. We leave behind a little of ourselves. You may doubt this. You may seek to believe that adage 'out of sight, out of mind'.

But let's consider this. Contact with another, be it good, happy, sad, or fruitful, is our imprint on society.

There are times we dread our meeting with a certain someone. We send out distinctive vibes of apprehension which, though cannot be seen by the opposing side, all our basic instinct tells us all is not well.

There are times when a happy outcome is predicted. Oh, how different is our concept of life, then?

Facial impressions, too, act as a warning. They lead us to believe little of what is really going on with our opponent.

Facial impressions, good or bad, can give us mixed messages. What the eyes see can allay our fears, but the spoken word is that powerful message of what is in our hearts.

So be ever watchful. A slip of the tongue is our downfall.

189

I once had a pony called George. He was all mine, and I loved him so. I knew I was very lucky. I guess my parents must have been rich to be able to afford him. I treasured him. I knew that I was the envy of all my friends. I was indeed very lucky. We used to go for walks along many a bridal path, George and me. We had not a care in the world. Life was good, and I was happy.

There came a turn of events that I could never have predicted. Mother got fired from her job, money became tight, and so as you can guess, George had to go.

Oh, that day I will never forget. The tears, the pleading and the final goodbye to my dearest friend. I was too young to understand. Oh, how I blamed my mother, how I blamed life for being so cruel. It was not fair. My life revolved around him. But he was gone from me, far away, never to be seen again.

We all have to experience this in our lives, the loss of a dear friend, someone whom we think we cannot live without. But we do. We carry on. We live, we breathe, and we go through the motions until we realise that we can cope on our own. We are not joined at the hip.

The strength comes from somewhere. That inner strength we thought had left us at the start.

Do not waver or bleat when the going gets tough and remember to draw on that inner strength that is yours. That God-given resilience that sees you through any major upset.

You are never given too much to bear, you are not expected to do this alone, and no one is, not even the giants amongst you.

This gentle reminder I bring to you, for in times of trouble, we forget who is on our side.

190

When I was a little girl in Ireland, I had many friends. We often changed our names when we pretended that we were someone else. A movie star, perhaps, a comic hero or the latest popular idol. Oh, we did laugh at the acts that we performed.

I used to be called Patricia but changed my name to Marie Lloyd, the stage singer. Oh, how I loved her voice. Sweet as a 'skylark', for that was her nickname.

Joseph pretended to be Roy Rogers with his white horse called Trigger. He wore a Stetson, a mask and had a gun with one silver bullet.

Mary, well, she pretended to be a better version of me, but I could always reach the top note. We had fun. It felt good to be someone else. In our innocence, we saw no danger in it, for it was all pretence.

But as I look around now, I see people (though grown up and in their adult age) still pretending to be something else, someone else. Do they not know the difference? Can someone tell them please to stop playing games, for you hurt people with your grandiose air of superiority?

It may sound strange coming from a child, for that is who I am, but I see clearly now some of you on the Earth plane still playing games.

Do you not realise that you are now grown up, that the pretence must stop? For you harm yourself as well as others? Be who your soul really longs to become.

Perhaps you are not aware of your predicament. Perhaps you are comfortable with your demeanour. See yourself as through a looking glass. Do you like what you see? Yes, I do.

But what you cannot see for yourself is that little voice that is but a whisper now but longs to become a roaring tide that only seeks to knock down that brick wall that keeps the real you prisoner.

Escape now, little voice, escape and be heard, for you have a much sweeter song to sing.

191

I thought today we would talk about those things that annoy us, plague us, irritate us, and test our patience until we could scream but are too polite to say so.

Ring any bells? A flush of guilt, and a sore subject? We are all human with human frailties. Let not one of you that is amongst us deny this situation.

Look around you at the people who live by you, close friends and family. Hand on heart now, which one amongst that lot would you wish to see long gone?

What is it about this person that only seeks to annoy you at even thinking of their name? Do you do your best to avoid them or hide when you see them approach?

What is it about you that they disapprove? Is there a guilty conscience hiding somewhere? Do they drain your emotions, leaving you tired and vexed?

What would you like to see, and what changes do you wish could take place? Do you see my point? Why wait for others to change when all it takes is for you to be the first to do so?

It may sound simple, but it will take courage to change the habit of your assumption. What have you to lose? Stop believing in 'anything for a quiet life'. You deserve better.

Perhaps your opponent waits for your challenge, or perhaps they are your greatest teachers.

192

I know this may sound a trite and feeble comment but look at your life today.

Do you greet this day with a smile, longing to jump out of bed believing that the adventure of a new day is about to begin? Or do you dread that ring of the alarm clock, wishing it would fail to go off?

The laborious thing called work, called commitment, becomes our master and yet what choice do we have? We need to eat. We need that new car and that foreign holiday.

Man needs routine in his life, for is that not a form of expression of who or what he is? Even a housewife has her days for shopping, cleaning and washing.

Routine is that unwritten law that keeps us balanced in our lives. Even hobbies and recreation lend themselves to a specific routine. Why, even the stars, the sun and the moon live through their own routine.

Routine can be boring, it leaves us with no choice for change, but there is order, there is constancy, and there is structure.

Without order, our world would collapse into chaos. Without structure, law and order would cease to exist.

There is a season for all things. For life, for death and for rebirth.

We are told to 'go with the flow' and accept all things, but to step outside our routine, to behave as naughty children, is that so bad? Is that for our learning? An escape route if we promise to return once boredom sets in?

193

I thought this day would never end, but it has, and I have survived it. I have concluded that the soul has a will of its own. The body may be weak, but the soul carries us on to another day.

How can we ever know death? How can we tell another that our life has become a burden to us? We see their faces when we try to explain, to talk about such a subject. If we have no fear, why should the weakest become the stronger?

Does not youth ever think that death is beyond them, that they will never reach old age?

A depressing subject, this is not, well, not in my eyes, for I have seen much of the glory that awaits you.

I share with you my story, for it may bring comfort to those who fear it. I know, for I, too, have experienced it.

Death has a beauty all of its own. A strange thing to admit, but I know that fear is the energy that only confuses us.

To be comfortable with the thought of death, to know and truly believe is a concept that comes from a contented and loving soul.

194

I was walking today down a busy street, maybe in your town or one like it. All was hustle and bustle, everyone going their separate ways, locked in their world and oblivious to all that passed them by.

I stopped to look and see their faces. It saddens me to see so many frowns. So blank were their expressions that they could have been robots.

We are not aware of our image. The one we portray to others. We would be horrified if we did. For the mask that we wear, that we hide behind, belies us.

Our appearance we try to improve. We all like to look our best, this goes without saying, but what of our insides? What improvement can we make there?

As people approach us, what air of confidence do we give off? Are we even sure of ourselves? Do we see ourselves as being approachable?

What would you do if a stranger smiled at you? Return the smile or frown and look puzzled? Confused by this, would you turn in puzzlement wracking your brains in remembrance of this person, convincing yourself that the other person was mistaken and not you?

Rightly or wrongly, in an instant, we judge a stranger. First impressions cloud our judgement, and the shame is ours.

Perhaps I misjudge you too. What would you do today or tomorrow now that you are aware of my findings? Return the smile, or be the first to give one away?

195

Many stories have been written and many songs sung about love, life and about growing old. Some begin very sentimentally, some with an unexpected slant, but they all end with a promise of things to come. What songs convey to us is a point of view we have not experienced for ourselves. Rightly or wrongly, it is for us to judge.

Many songs have lasted through the ages. Others, once popular, then fade away, never to be heard again.

'Life is a song worth singing', go those familiar words, an evergreen song that makes us stop and think.

'You hold the key in the palm of your hand. Use it', and so it continues.

Poetry, too, plays its part in reawakening us to life and the living of it.

Maybe someday you will write a song or compose a line or two of poetry on your observations of life.

Would you like to share your beliefs with another? Would you like to declare your findings to your children, your siblings and all who care to listen? Maybe you lack courage, believing philosophy is only for the learned, and you would look foolish.

Go on, give it a try. Speak your beliefs and pontificate as politicians do. You may be surprised who agrees with you, and if they don't, well, you are the braver for doing so.

Be not dismayed, though, if others jest at your remarks. You can hold your head high knowing you honour your truth.

To live by your truth and never be swayed by others is the rock you were meant to live on.

196

The day began well enough. Problems that I had in the past had all been resolved, and life for me was on the up.

The day was to be mine. My soul had been ignited with a spark that seemed to shine from me, a light that beamed brightly for all to see.

None could touch or harm me, for I was invincible.

Was I going crazy? Was I being deluded or kidding myself? But yet, I could not deny this feeling of euphoria.

When our energy levels soar, when life shines before us, and we see our star shining ahead, what have we to fear? Is that not a signal from a higher source showing us that victory is ours? That we are never alone in the darkness?

Look and see with new eyes now. Even in your dark days, try to see your star. It is there, believe, and it will be so.

197

I had a dream, a fantasy. It helped me through reality. A popular song, one that you know of.

Ah, dreams, what puzzles they set us. What mysteries, what riddles do they impose on us?

We have daydreams, which are of our own making, but night-time dreams, we have no control.

Do you like riddles, puzzles and conundrums? Dreams can appear so. Upon awakening, when the dream begins to fade, we desperately hold onto it, hoping it will not fade until we have fathomed out the message. The warning or the answer to whatever problem we are seeking is rarely clear to us. Rarely do we see and understand the message. We are fortunate if we do.

What is your dream? What is it that keeps hope alive for you? Have you asked for an answer? Do you expect one?

Don't be disappointed if no answer is forthcoming. Wait a while, and only when the time is right for you will you be given the answer. Maybe not in a dream, maybe not this day, but who knows, tomorrow that dream will come true.

He who answers dreams, he who speaks in riddles, and he who knows you better than yourself will grant all your heart's desires.

198

Ding-dong goes the bells; ding-dong for all to hear.

Ding-dong sings the bells; ding-dong for all to hear.

Ding-dong goes my soul; ding-dong sings my soul.

Ding-dong goes the world, ding-dong sings the world.

Ding-dong goes my heart, ding-dong sings my heart.

Ding-dong we cry out loud, ding-dong joins the band.

Ding-dong proclaim the news, ding-dong believe the news.

Ding-dong all join in, ding-dong let's all begin.

Ding-dong the Son is risen, ding-dong the birds all cry.

Ding-dong proclaims this day, ding-dong a bright light appears.

Ding-dong no more to grieve, ding-dong we are all relieved.

Ding-dong sings my soul, ding-dong in unison we proclaim.

Ding-dong my heart cries out, ding-dong around the world it rings.

Ding-dong a new day has begun, ding-dong a new battle cry is ours.

Ding-dong let all hearts rejoice, ding-dong blend your heart with mine.

Ding-dong the Angels sing, ding-dong the new day begins.

199

Who's that knocking at the door?' called the old man.

'It's only me', called the Angel. 'May I come in?'

'Why, what do you want?'

'I only came to seek shelter from the storm.'

'But there is no storm. All is well. All is quiet.'

'Please let me in. I am getting cold.'

'Go away, do not bother me. I do not need you pestering me.'

'I can't do that. I have only to wait to be invited in.'

'Please go away and leave me in peace.'

'Can't do that. I have my orders.'

'What orders? Who sent you?'

'Why, my master, God himself. He bids me wait on you.'

'What do you want from me?'

'Why, I have come to take you home.'

'But I am home. I do not understand.'

'I come to take you home. Please allow me to do so.'

The old man became concerned. Who was this trying to fool him? 'Go away. Why me?'

'Because, my friend, you are dead. I come to take you home.'

The old man ceased his complaining, and silence filled the room. Is this how it is? Is this the way forward? Gingerly he opened the door, and there before him stood the most beautiful figure he could imagine, holding out a hand ready to be accepted, ready to join forces on the long journey home.

The old man smiled. Yes, he was ready. His waiting was over.

200

Have you ever wondered why the Earth is the shape it is?

'No, not really, it just is.'

Have you ever wondered why day follows night?

'I guess it has to, for it would be either all day or all night.'

Have you ever wondered who you really are and why you appear to be alive in this century? No answer, no reasonable guess?

Was there ever a time you would have liked to be born into? The 18th century or the 19th century? Why now in this 21st century?

I see you ponder. Is it a question in your belief of reincarnation? Have you indeed been born many times over, and this is your latest one?

Who decides when we are born? Is this a choice of your parents? Did you have no say in this matter? Do not believe in chances. Do not be swayed by others deciding for you.

I see I set you a puzzle. Either you choose to live or remain in spirit.

Where does your soul come from? Do you even care? Do you think that control is taken out of your hand and it's all nature's doing?

Do not draw on comparisons from the animal kingdom. Theirs is another existence far removed from yours.

When a job needs doing, we call in the experts. We seek out the top man, so when nature decides on the next generation, she seeks out the people who will best serve mankind on the Earth plane.

She chooses the next scientist, the next discoverers, the ones capable of accomplishing the task ahead.

Do not be deceived into believing that you were born by chance. You have a purpose here right now, and that purpose is for you to find.

It may be something noble. It may be to make a great discovery, let's say, in medicine, construction or even just to 'mother' the next generation, for you have that capability. Never deride who and what you are. It is human nature to demean ourselves and see ourselves as less glamorous or less knowledgeable than 'so and so'.

You are here because you are needed in the scheme of things. You may be a small cog, or you may be a large cog, but wherever your place is in society, there you are meant to be, and the mechanics of society would not work without you.

Do not see yourself as anything less than necessary. You are here because the Almighty decreed it. You are here by rights. Let no man say any other.

201

If I had all the gold that's in the world, would it make me rich?

If I had all the rich resources at my disposal, would that make me rich?

If I had all the people worship at my feet, would that make me rich?

If I could hold humanity in my hand, could I make it better?

If I held the stars in my hand, would that make me any wiser?

If I could make your dreams come true, would you be any happier?

If I told you that you could do all this for yourself, would you believe me?

If I told you that the Earth and all that there is in it is yours for the taking, would you believe me?

If I told you my powers are your powers, would you believe me?

If I told you that all you have to do is believe me, would you listen?

If I told you that love is all the riches that you need, would you believe me?

If I told you that my love for you is all the riches that you need, would you believe me?

If I told you that soon man will learn this, would you believe me?

And if I told you that soon, you would believe it too?

202

Daisy was a little girl in my class at school. She was my favourite pupil. Though small for her age, she could hold her own in any argument. Bigger boys tried to bully her, but she had many tricks up her sleeve that left them with 'egg on their faces', so Daisy was left well alone.

This little sprout of mine grew up and left kindergarten. She blossomed at her next school, graduated and went on to college.

I lost track of Daisy, my little sprout. I expect by now, she is a scientist or a teacher, teaching her own little sprouts somewhere. I often think of her. Why I am not sure, perhaps she reminds me of myself when I was young.

Is there someone in your life who has made a lasting impression on you? Someone who just as quickly entered your life with a quick hello and then disappeared forever.

What had Daisy taught me? What was her purpose in entering my life and marking it with her particular stamp? I pondered on this. Maybe she was the child that I longed for, and maybe she had that same spark of resilience that got me through a tough period in my own life.

Small as she was, she made a lasting impression on me, an impression that I hope I can live up to.

203

As you may or may not know, the world you now reside in is the one you have created for yourself. Pain and suffering may be all around you. Grief and despair are yours for the taking.

How do we perceive this to be? What wrongs in our lives have we created? What judgement is being met out by the powers-to-be? Do we even deserve this? It was not our fault! Grief and despair are that dark place where no one wishes to be. Pain and illness only seek to trap us in a constant spiral.

Analyse your situation. See beyond the top layer, dig deeper into your psyche, and try and see what other problems lay there.

Is your body telling you something other than what is in your brain? At this present moment, we are wrapped in this cocoon of disenchantment, a feeling of helplessness.

It is hard to do. It takes time and the foresight of opening us up to another way of thinking. Be open to any thoughts that flash by you, any memory of a difficult situation you thought was long forgotten.

We heal on many levels. We hold pain on many levels, and it is when that layer of pain comes to the surface, then and only then does it materialise into the physical, as pain or an illness.

We scream and shout, demanding someone else to heal us. A tablet may help, an operation too, but, and this is crucial, why oh why did it have to happen to you?

204

There once was a man called Joseph. He was tall and lean, rather a loner, one would say. Though he was from a large family, you would often find Joseph wandering in the hills on his own. This was his life, and this was his pleasure.

He had no need for pubs, sports or games, people he thought were brash, loud and opinionated. His idyl was peace, freedom and space, uncluttered and simple.

People tolerated his eccentric ways, leaving him to his peaceful existence. At work, he was no different. He tucked himself away in the corner, happy to work alone. (I could go on describing this guy, this dear soul whose only wish was to be rid of the rest of humanity.)

The failing was not in him. He knew he was different. He accepted the fact that he was 'an odd bod'. No matter, I am who I am.

Old age saw a change in him. Something happened at one birthday celebration. All the noise and merry making became too much for him to bear, and he slipped outside, glad of the darkness and the quiet.

He was aware of a shadow just ahead of him. A man, no face, just a shape. He called out his name, 'Joseph is that you?'

'Yes, I am he. I am here. What do you want of me?'

'I come to explain. I come to talk to you, and there is not much time.'

'I am listening. Go ahead, what is it?'

'Joseph, my friend, I have waited much for you. A long time has passed between us. The time is now. The time for telling is upon us. I choose no argument. I choose no discord. I only choose to bring to you joy, joy in all its glory, in all its radiance. Joy, that word, that love, that glow that only comes to those who love themselves as much as I love you. See joy, Joseph. Feel joy, Joseph. Know joy. Taste it. Walk with me, Joseph. Let me into your heart and let the heaviness leave you. Throw away that black cloak of emptiness. Much you have missed, and much is there still waiting for you. Join with others, become one with the ALL. There is nothing to be afraid of.'

205

I look on you today. I look down and see the sad sight you all seem oblivious to. This is no reprimand or judgement. This is just the observation of a fool. A fool who thinks that maybe one day soon the eyes will open and you will see reality in all its glory.

This is not a test or a conundrum. It's the logic thinking of me, detached from you and all of mankind. I have patience. I need patience when dealing with stubborn, independent souls who seem hell-bent on destroying my beautiful creation.

Yes, you. You who seem to think that you are invisible. I remind you, you are not. Nothing is missed by me. Nothing that is seen or unseen ever goes unnoticed.

I often wonder why, what are you afraid of? Is the living of your life all too much, too heavy a burden for you? Carrying on believing that each day is a trial that must be won or lost?

It saddens me to see you thus. Is it a disappointment to you too? For life was never meant to be this way. I come just to say, just to give a simple message to you who despair, who live and blame all others around you for what is clouding your eyes.

Blink and be refreshed. Open those eyes and see again what can be put back to the way it was before. It can be. It's not too late.

206

What does a rainbow mean to you? Colour, sunshine after rain, the end of despair, or a sign of hope of a bright new day yet to begin? All these and many more. Consider the colours of a rainbow.

For instance, red is the colour of energy, anger, and danger. Red conjures up a feeling of heat. A heated argument, you may say, the heat of the noonday sun or the colour of blood and open wounds. A troublesome colour. An uncomfortable colour for some. A glorious richness for others, of royalty, pomp and ceremony.

Is the colour red a true colour or a mixed colour? Is it more of an emotion? Does it lend more to the outrageous extroverts that live amongst us, liking and knowing that they stand out in the crowd when wearing it?

Does red malign the wearer? Does it give that false impression of confidence?

How does red 'feel' when you say the word? Does it resemble power, dominance, and an attention seeker?

Do shades of red make a difference? Do you believe in the power of colour? Does wearing red empower you? Has it a vibration? If so, do you sense it when wearing that colour?

Take a red flower. Look at it, join with that flower, and let it consume you. Do you feel a change? Are you sensitive enough to hold its vibration? Despair not if you cannot.

For those of you that are drawn to the colour red as your moods change, know that all is well in your life and that no harm will come to you, for red is the colour of your Angel.

207

Orange is my favourite colour. Orange, for me, represents the sunset, warm poppies glowing in the field, and ripe, juicy fruit on the trees.

Orange has a glow about it. It vibrates with love and warmth.

Those of you who have a problem, a clash of personalities with this colour, only doubt your ability to see further than the end of your nose.

I jest not. Think about it. Stop right now and think about this. See a situation where you are in trust with a friend who asks a simple question.

They ask you to be honest with them, and they tell you this, so the last thing you want to do is to hurt your friend with your answer. (We have all been there.)

It is blatantly obvious that you must speak your truth, for your face will not hide what you are thinking. 'Trust me on this,' you say, 'Trust me, I know best.' Hold your breath for a moment. Hold them in your heart before you speak. Only and only then will you dare to give them your opinion.

You are on the orange ray. You know that what you have said comes from that place that only seeks to do justice to your soul.

208

Yellow comes next, the sunshine colour of happy days, summer holidays, golden weddings, and corn-coloured fields.

With yellow in our aura, we radiate the glow of victory, of completeness, and of being at one with the source.

Yellow is the colour of gold, that magical element which we long to possess. Be of good cheer all ye who are drawn to this colour. It is not greed that fills you, but a knowing, a deep connection with a glorious vibration. Do you not know why you do this? Does it set you a puzzle that vexes you until you give up? What makes you the person you are?

What person would you like to become? Daring, dashing, or a free spirit without a care in the world?

'If only', I hear you cry.

What if courage was your second nature? You would have no need of this vibration, for the colour you seek is the colour you lack.

Other colours may do for now, but are you going to be content with any colour? Are you willing to be ordinary?

209

Next comes green, glorious in its vibration. See rolling hills, imagine rain forests, and imagine spring with trees in bud. Green begets healing. Green knows a great truth. The 'green man' in his forest of fairies and elves. A hiding place for animals.

The green vibration is of re-birth and of a promise of things to come. It is energy, and it is life.

Those of you who are drawn to this colour know a great truth. You show to the world your understanding and your empathy with nature and her struggle.

Green, I salute you, all who realise the colour green. You are our warriors of truth. I cannot say it enough. I cannot emphasise my faith in you enough.

Judge not others. Judge not those who pooh-pooh this idea, for their eyes are not yet open.

To be born on the green ray is a gift indeed. Yours is a glorious life, the stuff of angels and the way of truth. But be aware of this, do not abuse it, for rays can be fickle and lost.

210

Ah, blue. Gentle, loving unhurried, cool, healing, Mother Mary, frosty days and clean.

Blue, for me, represents all that is 'Mother Earth'. All that is wholesome and true.

You may say that ice-coloured blue lacks any comfort and warmth and any feeling of love. We presume blue to be negative. 'Feeling blue', and 'Got the blues' when our day becomes a disaster.

Blue, as in all colours, has many different hues. In liking blue, you are at peace with life. You know your place in society, have no need to reach any higher, and contentment is yours.

'Blue skies' may not always be on your horizons, but without this colour ray in your life, how can you see beyond despair? How can you ever know hope?

Blue may not be the optimist's choice when it comes to believing in 'self'. It's the proverbial pessimist that clings to this ray. He knows no other, he seeks no other, and he chooses to believe no other.

211

Blessed indigo, that velvet blue of the night. Feel it, sense its richness, and sense its security into which you can hide. Indigo is that mastery of half-truths, not quite sure, and yet the mystery is ours if only we have the courage to see beyond the veil.

Indigo, just to say that word conjures up dark, mysterious feelings deep inside us.

Explore that word and that feeling that it brings to you. A reminder of dark star-lit nights, with only the moon to light your way. This sets the scene for stories of mystery, of wild images, and of ghosts and goblins, witches and fairies.

But do not let your fancies fly too far away. The reality is simply not so. For darkness begets the light, and light begets darkness. They are the same, just the reverse of your own self.

With light comes dark. It is so. It is balance in all things, for without darkness, where can we shine our own light?

212

Violet is the stuff of kings, the pinnacle and that crowning glory you are home.

Much more I cannot say except you may never know of this ray, for it takes another to see it in you.

Violet brings about a change in your persona, subtle but true. Once you have achieved, and your work on the Earth plane is done, it will not necessarily be a reward but the gratification of a job well done.

See violet in your mind's eye, feel that radiance, and sense its power. Power is all around it. The vibration that it portrays pushes you ever onward to your goal till you can hold that ray in your hand.

Violet, my dears, is there for the taking. Go and judge yourself not by your standards but by my standards.

So, my story ends. Dissect your own rainbow existence and see what colours your life. Treat them with respect, the colours you like and the colours you perhaps dislike but remember what colours your life shapes your life.

And oh, that glorious blend when they all shine together. Someday you may find your own crock of gold closer to home than you thought.

213

My dear diary, I come today to record the passing of a dear and devoted friend. For many years we have been companions, and many a long road we have travelled.

I grieve for the emptiness in my life. That hole, that gap that has seen fit to appear in my life. I know my reliance on this friend was wrong. I too, know that I should not have lived my life around such a creature, but he was mine, and I was his.

I look now and see with a tearful eye at my loss, for where do I go now? Who is there for me? What am I to do?

It seems to me that we pets are here for one reason only, and that is to be a plaything for humans.

Try as we like to survive without them, evolution has made this impossible. Once, we were independent of them, and we roamed the plains fending for ourselves. The old days will never come again. So here we are in the name of progress evermore to be lumbered with man.

Yet we dream. We dream of our ancestors, warriors to the death, meeting danger every day and not knowing where the next meal was to be found.

How times have changed. How much we have lost, yet who says, 'It's a dog's life?' I like being a dog.

214

I know what's wrong with you,' said Mother. 'At least I should, you are my daughter, and I know you better than you know yourself.'

How many times had her mother reminded her of it? All day and every day, it seems. Perhaps she did, but Mary knew she did not.

Habits, we all have them. We hear ourselves repeating word for word the echoes that were verbalised to us when we were children. We swore that we would never repeat them to our own children if we had any.

But history has a habit of repeating itself. We try to be logical and reason with our offspring, but someone has to be the boss. With the last word being in contention, we choose not to lose face.

Power is an emotive subject. Dominance over our rivals is all.

But what do we gain in badgering the less able amongst us? A feeling of superiority, aren't we clever? I've won again. Shame on you.

I say be gentle with them. Hold them in the palm of your hand. They will learn a much better lesson. There is no need to prove to them that you are the adult. It's proving it to yourself that matters.

215

Doubt is a funny word. Short and sharp.

D   is for disbelief

O   is for obstinate

U   is for uncertainty

B   is for belligerent

T   is for time

Does this sum up our world? It's good to doubt, it's healthy to doubt, and it's wise to doubt. It knows that just maybe there is an alternative.

Seek your answer and be sure of your answer. Then and only then will the doubter become the teacher.

216

I know a place far, far away from the hustle and bustle of my everyday life.

My special place is hidden deep within the woods. I found it by chance when I strayed off my usual beaten track. No one seems to know of it. It is mine, and it is special.

And why is it so special? It's because I know I am truly alone, truly at one with nature and myself. I would share it with you for you are my best friend, for you, I have told of it.

Don't betray me now, for you and I will share all I possess. We are friends, are we not? We like the same things, aim for the same things and believe in the same things.

Trust is vital. Trust is all in a friendship. We will never let each other down, for we rely on each other. You and me, me and you.

Who is me? Am I you? Or are you me?

Have you solved the riddle yet? Has the penny dropped?

You became me when I became you. We are the same. You are my reflection, that part of me. The two halves as in a whole. You look, I see. You hurt, I cry. You are happy, I laugh. We are never alone.

I remember, as a child, not believing in fairies. True, I did read about the coloured pictures of them in my drawing book, but if I could not see them, how could I believe in them?

A logical and straightforward question. Do not expect me to be persuaded by any glib reasoning.

I suppose I was born with an analytical mind, only believing what I could see and what I could prove.

I did well at school, calculations were my forte, and in maths and chemistry, I excelled.

I remember one exception to the rule, though. I had a Maths Master who set us a puzzle – how to measure our memories. We had to judge what was important and place them in order of merit.

Was birth more important than reading? Was walking more important than speaking?

I worried over this. Try as I might, I found it impossible to place a value on my achievements. He knew it was impossible. He knew we would all fail.

And the lesson that I learned? Well, here goes.

All is important. All that is seen and unseen is important. Just because it cannot be seen, just because no logical reason or visible proof is given, it does not mean it is any less true. The mind is capable of believing in the obvious, but it is our soul that knows.

218

To believe in a parable, to reason and understand the riddle of life is a mastery that is given to very few.

Do you ever look at a rainbow and wonder who or why it is so? Does it ever cross your mind at the wonder of nature? There is much in this world that we take for granted. There is much that becomes the ordinary everyday occurrence, and yet the marvel of it escapes us.

My dear reader, what would you give to be blessed with the foresight of the future? To see with untainted eyes at the wonder that can be achieved?

I look down at you now, not from a lofty height but with reason and a belief that all is not lost. To believe, to have a knowing that cannot be explained, and to know with a passion that only you can comprehend. A belief that come what may, you will survive, not beholding to another, never having to justify that grain of truth that you know that only others can look and admire from afar. A truth greater than your heart can hold, leaving others to envy your compassion and light, your certainty of a far better day than the one that has just dawned.

And who can hold this secret? Who is the guardian of them is blessed. Why is it not you? Would you believe me if I told you? Would your heart be at peace? Would you accept my gift?

I go to prepare a place for you. For in my Father's house, there are many mansions. Come choose one with me.

219

I know a lady fair of face and noble in her manner. She greets all she sees with a smile and a kind word. People leave all the better for being in her company.

Perhaps you know this lady. Perhaps someone like her lives down your road or resides in your circle of friends?

What makes the person behave in this manner? Is it natural? Do you find it irritating or comforting? Is it all pretend or all for show?

I ask a question, do you like people? Not just the odd one, not just close friends, but really like people? Do you find them interesting and see them as full of knowledge yet to be discovered? (It may seem an odd question, but it is vital to my thesis.)

Some of you I know long to escape from this world, believing they intrude on your time. But where would you be if no one knew of your existence? Alone on your desert island that no one wants to be on?

Next time when this little old lady greets you, haste not by her, for she teaches you a great lesson.

220

We sometimes take it upon ourselves to be the 'whipping boy' of others. Why do we do this? Is it a sense of duty or a calling that is placed on our shoulders?

Mothers are a prime example of this. We choose to shoulder the burden of our offspring to see that no danger or ill fortune befalls them. It is that martyr syndrome, that inborn survival technique that comes to the fore when our dear little ones are in trouble (not of our making) but of their own.

It is human to protect one's offspring. It is nature's unwritten law, and we have no control, nor should we do any other.

We, mothers of the world, who cherish our role in life, will raise heaven and hell to protect the new generation. It is our right that dormant strength that rises on such an occasion. The force of it scares us. It shows itself when we least expect it. This is a force that has governed the female psyche through aeons of time. It is that force that could turn the tide of humanity.

Female is a great and noble energy that sends shivers down the spine of the male. He may have the loudest voice and the greater strength, but it is the female who holds the key to survival.

221

Hark I say unto you, all that travel on this road of life stop one minute to accept this thought of mine. Where do you go, and why do you go?

The where and whys of life are many. The journey is long, sometimes tedious, and sometimes joyous.

What do you take with you as you journey? The hope of a bright new day? A day with sunshine when all of yesterday's problems disappear?

It takes strength to persevere and to do one's duty day in and day out. Oh, how we long to reach the other side when it all gets too much, when no one sees us struggle.

I know of the pride that resides amongst you. I know you are determined to see it through for just one more day.

As you struggle, as is the norm, what would you give to release the burden, the drudgery? A helping hand, an escape route, a trouble-shooter?

Look no further than Him, who walks beside you. All you have to do is ask. 'Shout it out loud, swallow your pride. You will be glad you did.'

222

This day has been a troublesome one, has it not? With its ups and downs and decision-making, do you feel glad that this day is drawing to a close?

Rest awhile and reflect on what this day has meant to you. You didn't mean to lose your temper, this we know. You didn't mean to shout at your little boy even though he tried your patience. You should have smiled and acknowledged the old lady across the street instead of hurrying by pretending you had not noticed her.

Does this sound all too familiar?

Deep down, you know that you are sorry. 'It's not like me. I should try harder. Oh well, tomorrow is another day. I'll try again to be the person that I really am.'

Familiar? I have been there, I know. My conscience pricks me even now.

We all hope that there is a tomorrow. We all hope and trust that we will see tomorrow. I bet you do. I didn't.

223

I look and see today as a day of decision-making. Big ones or little ones, they all matter. Choices in life, we all have to make them.

Choices can make or break you. Choices made today will affect all your future needs.

It can be scary, and it can be heart-breaking, but decisions, as in all things, are the necessary evil of life.

How do we sum up our decision-making? With care and attention? On the spot without a second thought? And what if we make the wrong decision, are we doomed for life? Care, as in all things, is necessary when contemplating our choices.

Do we look to others for help, believing they know our needs better than ourselves? Are two heads better than one?

I may know what you are thinking, all of you that have come so far in this book. The conclusion is obvious, so why do I waste your time?

Maybe some of you are not 'there yet', not ready to relinquish your power to another.

Be gentle with yourself. It's scary at first. You are right to be cautious. But if you ask the 'other head' for help in your choices. He will oblige.

224

We all wish on a star. We all wished when we blew out our candles on our birthday cake. We are all hoping for what – riches, a new job, a new fellow in our lives, a chance to be someone else, prettier, taller, better teeth, I could go on.

Step back a moment and see again with different eyes the glorious person you really are.

I ask you why you want to change. What demons do you possess that you need to change?

Vanity does not become you. You ask, not expecting it to happen, and if it did, would you be satisfied?

I think not.

225

Let's talk about children. Love them or hate them, they are here to stay.

There are times when we forget that we were once one of them. We all presume that we were never as awkward, as difficult, and as rude as the child that is standing here before us. No matter how we see them or try to avoid them, sooner or later, they enter our lives.

We may never sire a child, and we may never own up to deliberately needing a child in our lives, but come that what may, sooner or later, a child enters our family.

It may not be yours. It may be the fault of your sister or brother that you are to become an aunt or uncle (the ever-willing babysitter).

I love children, really, I do, but in small doses. I admire any grown-up person who relishes the company of young people (patience is their virtue).

A question. Do people have children for the sake of their own mortality? Do they see their children as a continuation of their line, a heritage that has to be passed on?

Children can indeed be a blessing. Many of you will agree with my statement. But has there ever been a time you wished them far away, a mistake that can never be rectified? Hand on heart now!

You see before you now a person who has this vision of the future. A future more glorious than you could ever imagine considering the state of the world as it is today.

Do not malign these youngsters. Do not laugh and ridicule their ways or their beliefs. They are learning as they grow in their years. Let them make their mistakes. Let them argue the toss with you, for it is in voicing their beliefs and frustrations that we know where we are going wrong.

For out of the mouths of babes comes the truth whether we like it or not.

226

Let us now dwell on a quieter and calm note. Let's visualise a sombre moment in this busy day of ours. All your work has been done, all is clean and tidy, and the rest of the day is yours.

Ah, bliss. Ah, rapture. At long last, the jobs to-do list has been completed. Freedom. But freedom from who or what? Are we our own taskmasters? Is there a hidden genie tucked away deep inside us that is only allowed out when we have been good and diligent?

Food for thought. Who says you have to be this meddlesome maniac that restricts your freedom and pleasure? Whoever it is should not be allowed to get away with spoiling your fun and freedom.

Tell them, or it, to go. You have no need of them anymore. You are free, you are your own person, and slavery has been abolished.

Are you so conditioned that the pleasure of freedom only co-exists from you being freed from your own habitual habits of drudgery?

Who is the master here, your own will or those of your conditioning?

'Freedom' is your battle cry. Away with pleasing others, the self knows, and the self will not waste your time.

227

A bat and a ball, a kite and a boat, that was all I could take with me on my holiday, more was not allowed – strict orders, strict discipline. Mother had to be like that. So many of us to care for and not enough time to do it in. It's not all fun being a member of a large family. It's not much fun being a member of a small family either, and the choice is not ours anyway.

Families come, and families split and go. That's life. That's how it is and always will be. Though distance between families, be it short or long, is not as important as the effort it takes to reconnect.

Do we seek them out when problems arise? Do we remember their anniversaries or special dates? Do we choose their company for our celebrations?

We grow up, we grow apart, we develop different needs, and our family cannot always fulfil our needs. No problem or quarrel, just the underlying feeling that we should be more tolerant.

We expect much more from family than we would ever do from a friend. It's not fair, and it never will be until we see for ourselves the hurt and embarrassment that we inflict on them.

We expect family to understand our plight. We can see no reason why they let us down or why they will not go that extra mile for us.

Blood is indeed 'thicker than water'. It was meant to be so that when we drink from the cup of life, we only consume enough to keep us buoyant.

228

I choose my thought carefully. I do not wish to alarm you, dear reader. It is with care and consideration that I do reiterate my story of woe to you.

I once believed that I was invincible. Nothing that was of this Earth or the next could harm me. How wrong I was. It may sound foolish, it may be trite, but I was told by doting parents that this was so.

How could they protect me, especially from myself? It was not that I was disobedient, I was just a little bit forthright and stubborn. (Forgive if I ramble, but this comes as a warning to all who think like me.)

The ego is that tyrant who rules us. We think not, we argue this so, but we are blind to his rule.

We choose as we all do, for are we not mere mortals, that we can say and do as we think is right?

We forget that 'chance' has a part to play. That though we are blinkered, we only know how to aim straight. The belief is this, have faith in your own strength, but try once in a while to see another's point of view.

Go now and ponder on my thoughts, dismiss them if you must, but remember nothing is forever and nothing can and will last forever. But aim not straight. Aim at listening, judging before you shoot your arrow.

229

I am like a river
You are like a river
We all flow as a river
We all seek the shore.

I am a river
You are a river
We are a river
We all journey to the shore.

We all seek the river
We all seek the shore
We all long to reach the shore
Where will the river take us?
Where will the river take you?

Believe in your journey for the river is you
We seek the waters that join with the river
We know the ocean lies not far
You know it too.

You see the ocean
We all see the ocean
Go find that ocean that leads us home
Back to the shore.

230

Chocolate, I love chocolate. Chocolate is that promise of instant pleasure. You know where you are with chocolate. As a child, chocolate was a treat, a reward for being good.

What rewards do we crave now for being good?

We all profess to be as 'good' as we can. We all choose to be good to one another, and kindness is our middle name.

When problems arise, when things go wrong and temptation gets the better of us, how do we feel then?

Who is there to punish us? An apology is all well and good, but the guilt sticks to us like glue.

How to clean ourselves and rid ourselves of the stickiness, it's not easy.

The conscience plays its part. It seeks us out, relentlessly picking at the spot.

To forgive oneself is the hardest thing we have to do. To earn forgiveness is just a thought away.

231

While on holiday in the Alps in Italy, I met a rather remarkable man. I thought him old for his age, a little weather-beaten with a little bit of a stoop in his shoulders.

We met one day while out walking in those wondrous mountains. As I overtook him on a narrow, rather than steep mountain path, we exchanged the verbal 'good morning' as is the usual custom of all fellow walkers. I continued on my way, not giving this gentleman a second thought, and never expecting to see him again.

The day was bright and clear with not much wind. A joy to be out roaming at my heart's content.

The day wore on, and the weather changed. One minute it was bright and sunny, not a cloud to be seen. The next minute, on a breath, the weather changed. The wind got up, clouds gathered, and a storm was brewing.

What to do, continue or go back?

Putting on warm clothing, I decided to go on. The rain began slowly at first, then a whoosh, down it came. The heavens opened, and I got soaked. How I wished I had returned to lower ground. Too late now. I needed shelter.

Luck was on my side, for there, coming into view, were rocks and shale. I was nearing a well-known set of caves locally known as 'the heaven sends', for indeed, my dear reader, they truly were.

To my surprise, who should be there, boiling his billy can, but my old compadre, the old gentleman I had met earlier. The smell of coffee filled my head with longing.

'Do stop and share with me,' he said. 'Please make my day with your company.'

It was an offer I could not refuse.

We talked awhile of other mountains that we had climbed and shared memories of triumphs and failures. It was time to go. The weather had improved, and the light was beginning to fade. He intended to continue climbing, and I decided it was home for me. Puzzled by his decision, I let him go. I said my goodbyes, knowing I would never see him again. We parted company, each following our heart's decision.

A long time passed, and the memory of that holiday faded too. One day, I happened to be browsing through some old photographs, and there he was. There in one of my photos, smiling at me, was the man whose name I had forgotten. It did not seem to matter. Not at all important. What was important was the memory that we both shared.

It seemed to me that throughout our lives, people come, stay a while, and then leave us. Are we the better for meeting them?

When an interlude is filled in our lives, when a chance meeting takes place, though it be for only a moment, the touching of another soul makes us realise that there is no such thing as a stranger, only friends yet to get acquainted.

232

Illness in our lives comes at a time when great changes are amongst us. Sudden illnesses come to us as a shock, as an intrusion into our daily routine of life.

What have we done to deserve this problem? What sins are we guilty of? Who is waving a big stick at us for being ungrateful and neglectful and punishing us for some misdemeanour?

We all resent illness. We all cry out, 'Why me? It's not fair. I don't deserve it.'

Illness comes when we least expect it, for no one expects to be ill. Accidents do happen, and sometimes it is our fault. This we understand. But there are many times when illness befalls us when choices are not of our own making.

How to handle an illness? It's not easy, it is painful, and it reminds us that we are not infallible. There are forces that we cannot control. Forces unseen take us by the hand and lead us to a place where we are meant to dwell. It may not be for long. It may be for the rest of our lives. We have no choice.

Illness is a state of grace that realigns us with the Source. It is an awareness that only seeks to remind us of the human factor of our frailty.

Illness is a struggle. It can be seen as a weakness in our human connection with our spirit. An illness borne with strength and resolution can be seen as a victory of our spirit.

Resent not your illness. See it as a challenge and see it as a test of your faith that only the outcome will decide your fate.

233

I know a place not far from here where all is peace and harmony. I go there when my heart is heavy with the cares of the day, of living in this busy world of ours.

You know this place too, you may have forgotten all about it, so I remind you.

'And where is this place?' you may ask. I refresh your memory.

It is that place deep within your soul, that space of peace and quiet calm. It waits for you. It longs to become your friend once more.

It only takes moments to reach that place. It is warm and cosy, and it is a haven, especially for you. Spend time there, take as long as you need, and go refresh yourself.

Close your eyes, and you are there.

PRIDE, my dear friend, is not such a bad thing and not such a good thing either.

Pride, as in all things, depends on your attachment to life and to others.

Pride in one's appearance is important. Pride in looking one's best gives us a sense of well-being.

But pride as in being 'proud' is of such vanity, dear ones, that I must stop you in your tracks.

To be proud and look at others as being beneath one's station in life is a sad indictment of one's upbringing. Just because one is born and raised on the 'right side of the track' does not mean that it is a condition of being superior to any other less fortunate.

'Money does not maketh man', so we are told. Being rich does not make us any superior to lesser mortals. Sad if you believe it to be so.

The rich and famous, how do you rate them? With envy, with longing and with a thought of 'if only?'

See beyond the trimmings, see beyond the glitter, and see only what makes you happy.

And would you swap it all for a big house with a yacht?

Ask your heart to answer that question.

235

ANGER. Anger – that dreaded affliction that creeps up on us when we least expect it. Without warning, it is there. Without thinking, words are spoken that we wish we had not voiced.

Anger can kill, anger can do such harm, and anger is a power that controls us if we allow it to do so.

Anger is ugly. Anger seeks to dominate our opponent. With anger in our psyche, we lose control. We let it control us.

Anger is regret. Anger only destroys, and anger seeks to intimidate. Anger is the last resort when all else has failed.

Anger is not real. Anger is only a thought form that allows us to lose control.

Anger is based on frustration. Anger sets out to be heard above all others, anger is raised voices, and anger is revenge.

Anger can be your buddy when self-respect has been taken from you. Anger only seeks to redress the balance.

Anger, whether good or bad, is our decision. Do not let anger control you. Do not let it dominate you. Stifle that wave when it begins to rise in you. Breathe out and release it through your teeth. Control it, master it, for indeed, it will master you.

236

ILLUSION. A complicated word with a complicated explanation.

Illusion conjures up mystery, puzzlement, questioning, and realms yet unseen.

An illusionist may bamboozle you with tricks and set your mind a-racing with his gift of confusion.

Illusion is, by its definition, a quandary. It sets us thinking that the impossible has just materialised in front of our eyes, and yet we cannot believe or understand why or how it happened.

The illusion that some live by is that we were sent here to struggle with life. They live in that illusion all their lives, never seeing what is behind that dark curtain the magician likes to use in his act.

Draw back that dark curtain on your life. See what is there on the other side. Don't go through your life under the illusion that this is all there is.

237

REVENGE. An ugly word. A destructive word. Revenge in all its darkness sets us aside from the animal kingdom. For to them, revenge is an unknown commodity.

Revenge is that gloating feeling that lingers deep within the heart of the perpetrator.

Revenge wallows in the pleasure of the deed. Revenge glows with the satisfaction of an alien form of justice.

Revenge will consume you. It will devour all other thoughts of reasoning. Revenge, dear ones, eats away at you like a cancer.

To seek and plot your revenge is a false pleasure. It is a false god that does not have to be obeyed.

What does revenge mean to you? The redressing of a balance and a righting of a wrong? Will revenge seek to satisfy you, proof that you cannot handle the hurt caused by another?

Blessed are those who walk away from hurt.

Blessed are those who feel a sense of pity for their assailant.

Blessed be you who can turn the other cheek.

238

I have a puzzle for you. Believe me or believe me not, your choice.

Why does a man who is strong and able only look to see as far as the end of his nose when crisis upholds him?

Why does he only seem to think that only his energy and wits will solve the problem?

Why do men seem 'hell-bent' on being a martyr to their cause? Is it not a victory to stubbornness or a winning of the ego?

He that thinks and believes that only his strength and tenacity can win the day is a bigot and a fool.

Did I hit hard? Do I hit home?

Can you explain to me why?

239

FREEDOM is a big and bold word. Freedom. Let the word ring in your head. How blessed we are to be born in a country where freedom is our right and privilege.

But freedom has its barriers. Freedom has its rules. To be free, true freedom is quite a frightening thing to be. For responsibilities for oneself are not for the fainthearted. Let me explain.

As children, we all long for freedom from our parents, from school, and from the old routine that we know. We daydream of that freedom, of the time when we are adults with no responsibilities.

Oh, how we were fooled. Once more our freedom is curtailed, the jobs, the mortgage, the ageing parents and once more, freedom is denied.

So, when are we free? When do we escape from these pressures? When we are dead? Is that our time of freedom?

We may never learn about freedom, we may choose instead a life of service, of caring for others, and will we have missed out on this glorious adventure called freedom?

I hope not, for come the day when we are free, it is then we commit to everlasting peace.

240

When I am hungry, I like nothing better than a hot steaming bowl of soup. I never get bored with soup. It never ceases to amaze me at the number of varieties of soup.

As I grew into adulthood, my taste buds changed. I moved on from the bland tomato and vegetable soup to the richness of mulligatawny, crab and sweetcorn to coq-au-vin.

Have you ever considered the similarity of soup to the human race? A bizarre thought? Let me explain.

Soup in all its glory is the zest of life. The combination of all the ingredients mixed together, all combined in a tin waiting to be opened up to the light and consumed.

Compare a tin of soup to the universe and to all of mankind. We are all tightly packed in the container we call Earth and the varieties? Oh, so many. Each one is different from the rest.

Where would you start to explain your taste in a soup? Mild and bland, or salty but well-spiced?

We all have different tastes in our choice of food and in our choice of jobs and lifestyles, so it should be. The comparison I choose between all of mankind is simply this, do not expect the flavour of your chosen tin of soup to be the same as that of your neighbour, for the difference is there for all to see. For the Lord your God so designed it.

Drink your soup, enjoy your soup, and compare not your choice.

241

TOLERANCE coupled with patience – we humans find it a heavy duty to bear. We reserve it for the saintlier souls who walk this Earth plane.

We know we should be more at ease with our fellow man, but why does it have to be me that is expected to be the one that 'carries the can?'

We all aim to be more tolerant. We know we should be more patient, but what rewards do we get for being so?

When problems arise and we know we are right and our opponents are so wrong, it's then we reach for that golden word, that state of righteousness. If only we could hold onto that space where our tolerance level resides, we know we can win the day.

Do not let it slip through your fingers. You can do it. Step inside that bubble of tolerance, and you will win the day.

242

I begin a new page today, dear friends, a new and glorious reasoning that only just now has come to my mind.

Is it not true that as we seek to understand this life, the whys and wherefores, the ebb and flow of our world, and all the challenges that are set before us, why do we take it upon ourselves to be born into this society?

Would it not be easier to become a recluse and to live one's life in a nunnery or a retreat far away from the hurly-burly of modern life? (Is it only a calling for the lucky few, the blessed and chosen ones?)

What have I let myself in for, taking on the demands of this world? What masochistic trait in me decided that this life is the best option? I deserve better. I deserve to be placed on a high pedestal, free from all the petty worries of this life. What foolishness did I believe at the beginning of my life that this would be my lot?

It's not anger that consumes me. I feel an injustice has been done to me by powers unseen. I choose fame and wealth, free from this mediocre life I lead.

This is not for me. I have been imprisoned in a wrong life. And yet, if this is my lot in life, is this what my destiny has decreed for me? How do I escape? Is there an escape? Do I have to wait another lifetime for my choice? Do I even get a choice?

But where I am is all that I am, and all that I am is Love.

243

There comes a time in all our lives when problems arise. Problems are sometimes of our own making, sometimes not.

How do we set about solving these problems? Do we worry, chewing them over and over again? Not sleeping, not eating, and snapping at our loved ones?

Do we dither over the alternatives, driving ourselves into such confusion that we do not know where to turn? By now, we are not capable of any rational thinking. Logic has passed us by.

Laying blame is of no use. Shouting is of no use. The problem gets heavier and heavier.

Compromise is the one solution. Adjusting to another's point of view, does that help? Does giving it 'time to heal' help?

Many suggestions and many remedies, but the best one may be the one you never thought of!

Have a word with 'Him upstairs', maybe he can help. You will never know if you don't ask.

244

Relationships can be difficult. I am sure you can give testimony to that fact.

In all families, whether large or small, we all are conscious of the difficulties of sibling rivalry. Parents, too, act their part out, sometimes caring and understanding and sometimes strict and severe, or so we think. We know that they have our welfare at heart, but, oh dear, why do they not listen to us? Why does it seem like a one-sided relationship? Do they demand our submission?

Relationships must be one of the hardest lessons we must learn. It's not easy, and we must work at it.

Relationships, as in all things, once mastered, becomes quite natural to make friends. The hardest part is keeping them.

What happens when relationships cease to be? What guilt do we carry then? Who is to blame?

Sometimes circumstances are beyond our control. Sometimes we out-grow the friendship. Sometimes our eyes are opened to their influences on us. It's no one's fault. It just happens.

Relationships come and go. People touch our lives for a number of reasons. Sometimes we understand why, and sometimes we are at a loss to know why they have to leave.

In relationships where the outcome is good or bad, lessons have to be learned, and we grow stronger for having experienced their friendship.

A relationship between parent and child, husband and wife, only seeks to cement a long-standing tradition of family life. We come together, we learn together, and hopefully, we come to an understanding, forming an everlasting bond.

Pressures in any relationship can become too intense and too demanding. When this happens, splits will form, breaks will happen, and the parting of ways happens.

Do we trust our relationships? Do we find comfort in knowing that we are secure in our relationships?

Friends can be our dearest form of relationship. People who love us 'warts and all'. With them by your side, we want for nothing more.

How do you see your relationship with people, family, friends and neighbours? A pleasure or a chore that society demands of us?

What would you say if suddenly you were cast amongst strangers, not knowing their language?

Scary stuff, eh? A smile will only get you so far.

245

A ticking clock broke his slumbers. 'Darn it, I'm late. Late again, the boss will not be pleased', and so begins his day.

Time. That elusive commodity that tests our patience.

We all consider 'time' to be given to us by some benevolent benefactor, an unseen force that we expect is our right and due, and yet we dare to be so complacent.

Time can be fickle. Time can play tricks with our memory, and time challenges us.

Time can be perceived as a long, continual line. People join in, stay awhile, and then fall off as in birth and death. (We are born, so the timeline begins. We grow old, we die, and we fall off the timeline.)

Time does not grow old. We who travel through time grow old, and time just 'is'. All creatures, all living plants, and all that exist in this dimension grow old. Time does not.

Time is continuous, time is repetition, and time is not ours to waste. Time can carry us into another dimension yet unseen. Time can be our future, as time can be our past.

Time belongs to no man, yet we expect it to be ours forever.

Time is now. Time belongs to the now, not to the morrow.

246

I saw you today, you did not see me,
   I saw you yesterday, but you did not see me,
   I spoke to you yesterday, but you did not hear
me,
   I will speak to you tomorrow, will you hear me?

   I will hold your hand today. Will you feel me?
   I will comfort you today. Will you allow me?
   I will try once more to be your friend. Do you
need me?
   I will always be there for you. When will you need
me?

   Trust me. I am your friend. Trust me, for I need
you,
   Trust me to be true, for I need you,
   Lean on me when there is no one,
   Believe in me as I believe in you.

   Turn not away when I call,
   Turn and look straight at me,
   Turn and see me for what I am,
   Turn and see me. Turn and return my smile.

247

RESOLUTION – a resolve to do better, a pact, a promise and vow to change, to become whatever we choose to be.

What resolution would you like to make? To stop smoking, to lose weight, those usual glib responses?

I know it's not New Year, but let's pretend that this is the start of your new year.

Where do you fail? What vices haunt you? Remember, no one is perfect.

It may be a small thing, some irritating habit that blights your character, or asks of others if nothing comes to mind.

Be patient with them, for they see the other side of you. Resolve to be all you can be, no matter how long it takes.

248

On the other side of the street lives an old lady who I see very little of. Weeks can go by until I see her. In my busy life I rarely give her a thought, until one day I noticed all her curtains remained closed, and this was by now mid-day. I grew anxious, not knowing what to do.

Should I knock on her door? Should I call a neighbour? I had no way of telling if she was in trouble.

It was then I realised just how little I knew of this lady, how reserved we are in our acquaintance.

Is this an underlining fault in our makeup? Is being too reserved a damning indictment of our generation? It saddens me to think that through my respect for her privacy, I failed to befriend her. I could have done more.

Do we as a nation hide behind this façade of no involvement because we are scared to intrude, or is it that no attachment is the best option?

They say, 'no man is an island', yet we choose to live on one.

249

I praise the Lord with all my heart and soul
His goodness knows no bounds
He leads me to my home on high
Where I am truly bound.

I know this may sound glib and trite, but at this moment in time, my soul soars with the love that I have for my Lord. In a small way, it is all I can do to praise his name. The hardest thing to do is to act it. But I will not be beaten, for it is my joy and pleasure to do so.

I came to realise that sooner or later, we all come to this understanding. No one counts how many lifetimes it takes. No one knows or sees when our eyes are opened. Only when we know deep in our hearts when gratitude pervades our thoughts, the reawakening of Joy.

Perhaps this has happened to you, or perhaps you await these awakenings? Give it time. There is no rush. There is no time span to learning.

I share this with you, though – believe not the ego, for it is a false god. It only seeks to trap us.

But who is this Lord my God? Is he some entity that seeks to brainwash us? Has he always been there hovering in the background, giving us a wave now and again so he is noticed? Am I vain enough to think that I am indeed blessed to be born into my religion? What does the word religion mean? The habit of lifetimes passed down to us by our parents? They say we choose our parents. Does this mean we choose our religion also?

What of other religions, do they miss out, never knowing my 'Lord?' It cannot be so, for I am no lesser mortal than the next one. The debate continues.

I leave you now to consider your own philosophy, for I am sure you know a bigger truth and see a bigger picture. But whoever is your Lord and Saviour, go in peace and serve your Lord.

Peace be with you.

250

TACT comes in all shapes and sizes. Tact is an art form. Once learned, it is the escape route from many a predicament.

To be blessed with this trait is indeed a gift, a quick and nimble brain that sees ahead of its time.

To be 'tactful' is to be aware and to be in the moment.

To be 'tactless' is the Freudian slip of the tongue that would see us being hung for shame. Difficult to judge, difficult to rescind and an embarrassment to all.

Tact, whether we know it or not, comes when we place another before ourselves in any given situation. The comfort of others is our utmost thought.

He who is blessed with tact is indeed the peacemaker. And blessed are the peacemakers.

251

Just one more time' is all I ever hear. 'Just one more time to forgive and forget. Just one more time, I promise. Give me just one more time.'

How can I refuse? How can I not forgive? What hard-hearted soul cannot understand the pleading of a child?

I look and see my dear children. I look and see about my world.

Forgiveness comes at a price. Forgiveness binds us to the forgiver. It can be seen as cementing a bond and atonement of friendship. The bond we have with another is strengthened and everlasting. It's a promise to believe that we have a future together.

Forgiveness does not glorify the perpetrator. The act of forgiveness is simply a knowing of better days to come.

And come they shall, my dears. Come the day when all know that forgiveness is the art of loving.

252

I am aware of you who read this book. I am aware of why you read this book and blessed be your hearts in doing so.

We all look for answers. We all have a need for others who may help us. We are not lazy or stupid with little knowledge to call on. No, we are here right now on this very day, on this very page, to seek out validation for what we long for, an aid in our journey home.

We acknowledge others have been here before us, much wiser and more learned than we are. This we accept, and in doing so, we continue this tradition of treading in their footsteps.

But has it ever occurred to you that maybe you are the next Ascended Master, the next one we all turn to? Stop believing in your smallness. You are more than a 'grain of sand'. The mortals you hold in such high esteem were and are just like you. They lived and breathed the same air. They walked the same pathway as you are doing. What is the difference?

You may argue that books have been written about them and a record of their opinions have been recorded, leading to their fame.

Indeed so, but what mark will you leave behind? Will others follow in your footsteps?

It only takes one person to see the good in you, and then you become that master, the teacher, and the example to live by.

253

TRUST. A small word but a big commitment. Trust has to be earned. It cannot be bought.

Trust is responsibility. Trust is being the guardian of someone's secret.

Trust is dependability, another's honour.

To acknowledge trust in another is to see them walking with giants.

To be called trustworthy is a compliment of the highest order.

See trust as a gift, see trust as a right that is ours, and see trust as a compliment that is paid to you by your Father. For 'trusting in our own righteousness', we may walk with him and he with us.

254

I am beautiful, do you not think so? I have a beauty that befits a princess. I have grace and beauty that befits nobility. Do you not see it? I am all that I long to be.

And who am I that asks such a question? Do you not know, do you not see? Pick up a looking glass. What does the mirror say? What does it show?

'Why only little old me. I see no beauty there. I see no regal air of grandeur.'

Are you sure? Is it only a mask that hides all that I observe?

You frown. 'Not so. It cannot be. Vanity is not the name of my game.'

Indeed not, but I do not play games. I see behind the mask, I know what is behind the mask, and others see it too.

Do not be blinded by obtuse thoughts. Look beyond vanity, be kind to yourself, and see the glory that is you. Others do.

255

There comes a time when all men must make a stand when their conscience tells them that a wrong has been committed.

Bravery may not be your strongest point, but still, you are not a coward, so somewhere you lie between the two.

Courage is more than a word for bravery. Courage comes when we feel strong enough to 'right the wrongs and go out on the edge of a crowd, out with a shaky limb'.

What would make you stand up and shout for another or walk that last mile when all had given up?

Making a stand is all well and good, but you put yourself up to ridicule. Could you face that?

Are you strong enough to hear the words of scorn of others? Does another's opinion of you make you blush and run for shelter?

The choices we make in life, all the decisions we live and believe in, are there for all to see.

All will notice our mistakes, and all will point and stare, but if you justify your beliefs, then no man can call you a coward.

256

A laugh a day keeps the doctor away.

A story once told is a story shared.

A belief is only a belief if the believer believes it.

Doubt another, and you doubt yourself.

A truth that is spoken is only true if you believe it.

Look and see the good in another, and you see the good in all.

Reason out a problem, and the problem becomes the reason why you doubted it in the first place.

Believe not others unless you believe in yourself.

Trust only when you believe others are wiser than you.

Forget not those of you who seek to travel far, for one day they may return to you, and where will you be?

Why waste time, for time is wasted on you.

He who sees the future is a contented soul.

If you believe, then you have hope.

As I see it, maybe not the way you see it, but let's compromise.

257

Holidays are good for you. Holidays are supposed to restore one's health, relax us and give us a break from our daily routine of work and monotony.

Holidays come and go all too quickly. Just as we get into the swing of our new life, we find ourselves homeward bound. Once home, the stress of unpacking and wondering why we ever did it in the first place leaves us, and we plan for the next one.

What is it that pulls us to a distant shore? Is it just the sand and sea? Is it the need to explore ancient monuments, trek up and over mountains and see wild animals in their native environment?

It is good to be inquisitive. Man has a need to learn and experience other cultures.

What do we hope to achieve when we go on holiday? A suntan? A fulfilment of one's dreams? Many reasons, and they all make sense.

What about those who fear travel and have never set foot outside their own hometown? Is it contentment that keeps them home? Is it just that life for them is complete?

We all have our reasons when choices are to be made. There is no right or wrong.

But whatever your needs are, they are right for you.

258

Is there a piece of music or a tune that you continually hum that will not let you be? It's there, just there, annoying and puzzling you as to its title?

Where did it come from? What links it to you? Why did it latch onto your subconscious? What memories does it conjure up?

Who sang the words? Who wrote the music? Why, oh why, has it latched onto me? I am at a loss. My memory knows, but I do not.

Is it help that I need? Is it a wake-up call?

Someone other than me is relaying a message that I am not getting. No matter how I puzzle it out, it will not leave me.

Why can I not see it? Perhaps I need help from another. Do you know this tune? Shall I sing it for you? Perhaps you are my connection. Perhaps together, we can fathom it out. Listen to me. I shall sing my song to you, and if you know the words, please join in.

For were we not born together? Were we not connected at birth? I have forgotten. Please remind me why I am here, why you, too, are here.

The words are simple, the tune sweet. I only need you to remember how to sing my song.

259

Jesus wants me for a sunbeam to shine for him each day. In every way, try to please him at home, school, and play. I'll be a sunbeam for him.'

Now that I am older and perhaps wiser, I look at life through different eyes. Jesus is my Guardian Angel. This I know without a shadow of a doubt. Without him, I would be lost. But Jesus is but one of many prophets that have come to Earth to guide and protect us.

I have a problem in that my belief is strong enough to be dissuaded into believing that he is the one and only true Son of God.

Many religions have their own prophets, Mohamed is an example. Is he any the less enlightened being than our Jesus? To judge another as being less able is as narrow-minded as it gets.

I do not intend any offence. I do not seek to trouble you but simply point out to you my philosophy. Believe it or believe not, it is your choice.

But this I add, be not blinkered in your beliefs. Is your faith the one and only true faith? How can it be when the world is so diverse in tradition and culture?

Bear in mind this one thought, why were you born in your country of origin? What difference would your life have been to be born into a 'heathen land'? Do you get my point? Who is the heathen, them or us?

260

And so begins the day anew. Sunshine, birds singing – it must be spring. Jobs to do, places to be, what a busy world we live in.

Would we have it any other way? Is there a purpose to our existence?

The purpose is to live each day as if it were our last. Is that so? Is that your belief? What about planning for one's future? Is that a waste of time? If so, it's a contradiction to my previous statement.

So is your life a busy one with lots of distant plans to be fulfilled, or a sleepy 'come what may' existence and does it suit your purpose?

One could envy the other. One borders on stress, the other on boredom.

Balance, as in all things, is the secret of success. Balance contradicts the stresses of your everyday existence. Time out is the antidote.

The problem is remembering not to overdose on either. The problem is knowing when to just be.

261

It all began one day not so long ago when William, a young boy rather small for his age, was on his way home from school. This little boy had often walked this way home, for the shortcut was always the easiest. He had never noticed before now that a cat lived further down the alley. (He loved cats, in fact, he loved all animals, and he intended to become a vet one day.)

The cat eyed him with mistrust, for he remembered other young boys and the pain they had caused. There was something about this young fellow that he liked. He had an air of trust about him. Yes, this is one to be trusted.

Approaching, William observed the stare of the cat. Perhaps we could be friends. Perhaps I can gain his trust. If these two souls could read each other's minds, how easy life would be. If only we could read each other's thoughts, if only our senses were so developed to do so. What a difference it would make.

How easy our lives could become to know in an instant what another was thinking. How careful would then be our perception of another? How easily honesty would sit with us.

If only life was that simple. If only we could regain our innocence.

262

This Gift I give to you
This Gift is all I can give to you
This Gift is mine to give
This Gift comes with love
This Gift is all my love
I give you this Gift of love.

May all who know you return your Gift
May all who love spread your Gift
May all grow to love this Gift
May the world one day share your Gift.

263

There once was a wise and noble lord who thought he had it all. His wisdom on the ways of the world was renowned throughout the land.

People would come to his door for guidance and understanding on points of law. He believed that he should be king and that he should be the one on the throne. For did not people worship at his feet, at his fountain of knowledge?

Conceit is the price some will pay for their actions. Conceit rides heavily on the conscience of others. My dear friends reading this book would never be accused of such a sin. I say this tongue in cheek, for to err is to be human. Guilt we are all guilty of, and yet we blush at the thought of being called so.

Conceit is a judgement others place before us. Conceit sits well with some people. They think it is a compliment.

I lay before you this thought.

When the ego rears its head, when vanity becomes our theme tune and when we fail to recognise the victory of others, cease the competition. Refrain from being 'top dog'. Step aside and just be. Let it go, see others in their glory, and all will see the glory in you.

264

My topic today is the big, bold word of co-operation.

The dictionary says 'co-operation' is a joint venture, a blending of souls who seek the common good.

Co-operation may be an assumption that the perpetrators of conflict have little choice when resolving matters of conflict.

Co-operation denotes a feeling of reconciliation, a need to compromise without losing face.

Co-operation in all things leads to harmony. A feeling that we all like to please, to be seen as amicable to our fellow man.

I do not intend to sound glib or contrite. I look and see that some assume that victory over another is a triumph. To be dictatorial is aggressing, and co-operation is compassion.

As in all things, treat others with respect, that in believing co-operation exists, compassion is love.

265

I know this may come as a surprise, as it did to me, but the consequences of our actions account for many of our problems. Problems we thought were not of our doing. Problems caused by others.

We shout and scream when we are let down by life, as is commonplace to do, but I urge you to consider a different thought-form.

Stop and reconsider why it has happened. Sit awhile and contemplate your lot. Can it have been a result of words spoken to another in haste, with venom from a lower part of you? In your haste, did you not consider another's feelings? Did you seek only revenge?

The pain we cause with another will, and I emphasise, will always rebound back to you. It is a true saying, 'He who casts the first stone should never live in a glass house.' For as sure as night follows day, your world will come crashing down, and all will rebound back to you.

Be aware, my dear children, be aware of your actions and thoughts, the power you hold, the power you project is lethal, and casualties can be many, and you may become the wounded one.

So beware, the bullets you send our way will always bounce back and be returned to you, for you are in danger of becoming your own worst enemy.

266

The birds are singing it must be spring
The daffs are blooming it must be spring.
The days are longer it must be spring
So where is your heart now that it is spring?

Does life for you now begin?
Does all seem hope now the promise begins?
Does your spirit rise with each bright new day?
How I wish with all my heart that it would stay.

So winter is gone, let all care subside
Greet this new era with love to reside.
Greet and be blessed as the Earth awakes
Let all who believe now make haste.

Never again to see dark days
Never know misery and heartache.
Never again will see doom and despair
For the Lord your God knows when he holds
your hand with care.

Let not dark days ever again reside in your heart,
Let not grief and despair your master make.
Look, see now the sun has arisen
Look, see now hope of a new day risen.

267

Joe Soap, that well-worn adage, a Mr Nobody, a John Doe, need I go on? These names that mean nothing to you or I.

What is a name, your name, and my name? Only a title, a sound that is given to us at birth.

Where do all these words come from? Who makes them up? Who chooses them, and what rights to these words do we have? A name, a number, seeking out of the individual.

Blessed be all who honour their God-given name. Blessed be the vibration that is you. Blessed be all who honour their God-given name, for the Lord your God not only knows your name, He knows what is in your heart too.

So be joyous when your name is called out by those who seek you. Be not abashed or vain, for your name has a beauty, a vibration that is you as much as you are it.

268

There are many words in the dictionary that have little usage to present-day speak, words that may seem outdated to the youth of today.

Vocabulary – are we conscious of the language we use? Is each word that is spoken carefully weighed up before it is uttered?

Slang – is merely a shortened version of the true word, a local colloquialism, and the new 'in' word.

Speech – is what we judge another by. The emphasis we place on our punctuation, and the phrasing of our words, all leave a lasting impression on others.

Speech – whether it is our friend or enemy, it is necessary to everyday functioning. Be not dismayed when your words are not heard. Perhaps you function on a different wavelength from others. But be persistent in your views. Perhaps the next time will be the right time.

269

I give this day to you as a token of my love. I look and see the deserving amongst you. I look and see the souls who grow and learn by their actions. This is their just reward.

I look and see all the others. I smile and see them struggle so. If only I could reach them, if only they would ask of me, then lighter their hearts would become.

Your days are indeed numbered, for it has been written so. Revenge is not mine to seek. The taking of a life is considered kindness to some. Taking back your days on Earth will be seen by some as unjust, but who is there to judge the rights and wrongs of such an action?

So, bless this God-given day, be pleased at your reward, and fill your day with joy at being just you. For many are truly blessed with this knowledge and others? Well, maybe one day!

270

Quotations are born out of the necessity of quick reminders of hope and our folly.

We remember them in times of trouble when wrong decisions have been made. When the soul is seeking consolation of the folly of its way or when a hasty judgement has been made.

Quotations are usually recorded by the learned and wise ones. They have been handed down from father to son, forever onward, warning each generation.

Perhaps you have your own quotations. Perhaps you have insight into some enlightened beliefs?

Are you willing to share? Are you brave enough to give advice?

It's not important that others listen. It's not believing that others are worldlier than you. It's knowing that without a shadow of a doubt that the words you iterate come from the heart.

271

Joy be to you this morning.
May joy be in your heart and soul.
May joy be there for all to see, reflected in your soul.
May joy be the light that shines from your eyes.
May joy light your way when grey skies prevail.
May joy see you through your days ahead.
May joy be yours when love rears its head.
May joy replace the pain that others inflict.
See joy as your right, see joy as your aim.

272

There comes a time in our lives when we must make recompense for all the wrongs and injustices that we have caused throughout our lifetime. It may seem like the end of your days, for youth sees no need in doing so.

As age begins to sit heavy on our shoulders, we begin considering our lives. The wrongs we have all borne, the missed opportunities with regret and the wondering if we would do it all again.

Would we do it all again? Should we dare to do it all again, or are we sick and tired of trying?

Each of us sees life differently. We have all had our share of struggles, headaches and disappointments. Have they been outweighed by joys and blessings? Is it only the downside of life that comes to us in our hour of reverie?

Choices are not always ours to make. There have been many times when fate has undone all our good intentions. And yet we soldier on, believing with hope in our hearts that it was not all bad and that perhaps tomorrow will see a better day.

And this is what we must do, not simply 'make the best of a bad job'. Indeed no, for your life is all that it can be. If not, why not?

273

The Earth, as we know it or are led to believe it, is ours for the taking. Whatever is deposited in the earth is ours for the taking. Who is there to argue with us? Who is there to say, 'nay not allowed?' The sea and all that there is in it, likewise.

Fish is meat to some. Whales produce oil for our skins and shells as ornaments, do you understand me?

Is the world ours to plunder? Is man the owner of such a wondrous object? Look to your hearts. Look and see. Are trees only there for shade and fuel? Is the golden black liquid only there for our means of transport?

Does nature provide only our immediate needs? Does she not try desperately for you to see what your soul needs?

She tries, oh how she tries with abundance if only you would wake and see with your inner eyes.

If you must destroy, please replace.

274

The tree that you sit beneath, the ancient one that has stood the test of time, why is it still there?

Is it a quirk of nature or a chance happening? Did man mean to plant one there, or are birds to blame?

Think a moment on this thought and consider your verdict.

I see you smile. Yes, what would we do without trees?

275

LAUGHTER, I bring to you today. Laughter, that joyous sound, that crackle of spontaneous energy that sets our hearts alight.

We cherish distant memories of occasions when laughter was shared with friends, with an audience, or on a page in a book.

Laughter brings us together. A cementing of like-minded souls. Who amongst us is not infected by a baby's giggle?

Why, my dears, do you then choose the other options? Why does the feeling that you so deny remain as a last alternative?

He who sees the funniest side of life is indeed blessed. He, who is the clown, is your greatest teacher.

To cry with laughter, laugh until it hurts, is to know life.

276

When we lose a dear and cherished friend, a hole in our hearts appears. A hole that we know will never be filled by another.

What is life telling us? Are we dependent and show a lack of our self-confidence? For without their support, we are lost.

We are given a test. We are being shown not only our strengths but also our weaknesses.

Does your memory at this time flood back to other friends now long gone? You survived, and you will survive again.

We know they are special, not like all the others, of this, are you sure? Life will never be the same without them. That is why they came into your life, to share, to dwell, and then leave. Leaving behind memories and lessons. But in your heart is where they will remain.

Be sad for a little while, wish them well on their way, and then cherish the more all who are left behind.

277

Let's begin this day with one thought in our minds, that this day is to be the best day that we have ever spent. Everyone is our friend. Everyone knows us as we know them. Let your heart sing at just being YOU.

The doubters, the grouchy, and the saddos be gone. We have no need of you, this day is ours, and no one is going to spoil it.

Whatever your plans, be it on your own or with friends, do as your heart dictates, for it is now in command.

The sea of life is yours for the taking. See with new eyes any problems that lurk around waiting to be solved.

How do you feel about my challenge? I dare you. I double dare you to give it a try.

If you do, I guarantee you a day like no other, the day you were born to live. See how quickly this day will pass, and then perhaps you will give it another try tomorrow.

278

As evening approaches, the body and mind realise that the day's work is done and slowly begin to wind down. The day's work has been done, and what is left undone can wait until tomorrow.

As in all of our God's creatures, they, too, settle for rest.

'To sleep, perchance to dream' ah, to rest in one's own abode, to know that all is safe and at peace.

The world quietens down, even traffic has lessened, and a glorious peace settles around us.

We have earned this rest, for we know that we will have to do it all again tomorrow, and yet we know we are truly blessed.

For what is man but an instrument of the Lord, a loyal and loving master who is our pleasure to serve.

279

LONELINESS is a cold and dreaded situation that we all fear. We think this will never happen to us, for we will ensure it does not happen to us.

Loneliness is never feared by the young. That word is not in their vocabulary.

Loneliness comes in the dead of night or in a crowded room surrounding you with laughing people. Loneliness becomes your enemy.

Why do we fear loneliness? Is there a difference between loneliness and abandonment?

What has brought us to this state of mind? Are we perpetually reminded of 'what if' we are left behind in a crowd? Others go and desert us? Is it only an ageism thing, a fear of being so old that all who we loved have gone and left us behind?

How do we save ourselves from this dreaded affliction? Who is there to comfort us and to tell us that it is only our lack of self-worth that keeps us from becoming that contented soul?

And the difference between loneliness and contentment? Why it is simply knowing our self-worth. So, fear not, for it will not happen to you.

280

Come what may, I will always love you.

Come what you do not see, that we are tied together,

Come what may, the bonds that tie us will never be severed.

Come what may my truth to you, I now relate.

Come what may, no one will see, no one will separate.

Come what may, my strength is yours to command.

Come what may, the love we share will never die.

I touch the stars, my universe grows.

Come what may, come share it with me.

The unseen shadows, the feeling of bliss

To you I command, come share with me.

281

The days grow long, evening is with us,
I call to you on the evening breeze
Be at peace, be at rest, for the day's work is over
A day well spent, a day of achievement.
I touch you gently on your brow
I soothe your aching back.
Well blessed is this day
Well done by your day,
Rest for you are spent.

I touch your heart,
I see you smile
You know that I am near.
You know without seeing me,
You know that all is well.
You know my dear friend
You know I am always here,
You know, you just know.

282

The sunlight came filtering through the window, and it disturbed her sleep.

'What a bother, it's too early to rise. It's sleep I need. I was sure I had closed the curtains so tightly. This was not supposed to have happened.' So, sleep became her friend again.

Are your curtains on life tightly drawn together so tightly that you live in darkness? Would you dare the sun to penetrate those thick black sheets of doubt?

Beware the sun, I shout it out loud, be aware of the sun and live.

283

The dream I had last night reminded me of you, my friend. No, it was not a horror story. It was a peaceful and loving memory that we once both shared.

I look back with gentle nostalgia when we were young, lost in our innocence and youth. Has time really gone so quickly? Did we deserve all that happiness and pleasure?

In our adult age, the longing returns to go back to what we once shared. And yet would we if we could? We were young and foolish, but those days were good. And what have we now? What has life left us with?

Memories, but what bitter-sweet memories, my friend. No one can take them from us. They are ours. I bless the adventures we travelled on and the days of sunshine that seemed to last forever.

To you, my special friend, to you, the light of my days, may the love that we shared never leave us, for eternity is ours.

284

I know I have said it many times and will say it once more 'All who believe in me, theirs is the kingdom of god.' Some may ponder this statement. Some may only believe in those pretty words for a moment and then pass them by.

I ask you to ponder this statement and consider what the words mean. Is it too much to expect it to be true? Too great a gift I give you?

Consider why I am offering you this gift. Ponder and consider the alternative. If your judgement considers the latter, then all is well, but if not, then what?

I give you a life that continues after death. I give you a future much greater than your expectations. I come to give you a reminder of all things. Consider why I do so.

Consider and believe it to be true.

285

My Granddad loved me, for he told me so,
I loved him, and I told him so,
My Grandad was old, he had wrinkles
But I loved him so.
He never shouted at me, he never told me I was
naughty,
For this I loved him so.
My Grandad was old, but I loved him so,
I want to be like him
And I told him so.

286

Perhaps today, as you look and see with eyes so young that the world you live in is not to your liking. Perhaps you would love to change this, change that, treat others differently, and set to right all the wrongs in this world of ours.

How you bleat your woes. How they seem to fall on deaf ears. You feel a sense of frustration. No one listens anymore, for what does one so young know of such things?

You believe the life you were born into was not of your making. Others are to blame, so what chance have I?

The world progresses at an alarming rate, and you do not want to be left behind. But you hesitate. You are loathed to join this rat race, this survival of the fittest and the cleverest.

In your innocence, you know there is more. There has to be more. You are sure there is more 'but where do I go to find it, this hidden alternative way of co-existing with my fellow man?'

Let me be the first to show you and point you in the right direction.

It is simple, believe in what you know to be fair and just, to be honourable in your attitude to your fellow man. See him as you are. Just know that he, too, is trying to bring this world of ours into the 'light'. Trust and know it takes only one to begin the revolution. Be all you can be. Go bang your drum so others may hear you, so others may follow.

Printed in Great Britain
by Amazon

27204167R00229